A word about th
Toastmasters Ir

Who needs another book on public speaking, let alone a series of them? After all, this is a skill best learned by practice and "just doing it," you say.

But if practice is the best solution to public speaking excellence, why is this world so full of speakers who can't speak effectively? Consider politicians, business executives, sales professionals, teachers, trainers, clerics, and even "professional" speakers who often fail to reach their audiences because they make elementary mistakes, such as speaking too fast or too long, failing to prepare adequately, and forgetting to consider their audiences.

As we experience in Toastmasters Clubs, practice and feedback are important and play major roles in developing your speaking skills. But insight and tips from people who have already been where you are might help ease some bumps along the road, reinforce some basic public speaking techniques, and provide guidance on handling special speech problems and situations you may encounter. The purpose of *The Essence of Public Speaking Series* is to help you prepare for the unexpected, warn you of the pitfalls, and help you ensure that the message you want to give is indeed the same one the audience hears.

This series features the accumulated wisdom of experts in various speech-related fields. The books are written by trained professionals who have spent decades writing and delivering speeches and training others. The series covers the spectrum of speaking, including writing, using humor, customizing particular topics for various audiences, and incorporating technology into presentations.

Whether you are an inexperienced or seasoned public speaker, *The Essence of Public Speaking Series* belongs on your bookshelf because no matter how good you are, there is always room for improvement. The books are your key to becoming a more effective speaker. Do you have the self-discipline to put into practice the techniques and advice offered in them?

I honestly believe that every person who truly wants to become a confident and eloquent public speaker can become one. Success or failure depends on attitude. There is no such thing as a "hopeless case." If you want to enhance your personal and professional progress, I urge you to become a better public speaker by doing two things:

- Read these books.
- Get on your feet and practice what you've learned.

Terrence J. McCann
Executive Director, Toastmasters International

"Karen Lawson has captured every technique imaginable in this comprehensive, practical, hands-on guide to connecting with your audience. From ice breakers to visuals, and from preparation to room set-up, if you adapt the ideas in this book, your audiences will give you rave reviews."

— *Elizabeth Jeffries*, CSP, CPAE, Professional Speaker, author of The Heart of Leadership

"Karen Lawson has given us lots of how-to-do-it insights and has answered many questions. Her clear writing makes this highly useful information easy to read. Anyone who desires to be an effective and efficient speaker will welcome this book as a handy reference."

— *Victor Costa*, ATM, Toastmasters International Accredited Speaker, President of The Victor Organization, Stillwater, OK

"This book is full of cutting edge ideas you can use immediately to bring your training and presentations to life. These techniques dramatically increase both the quantity and speed of material learned, and makes the experience enjoyable and fun."

— *Brian Tracy*, CPAE

"This is an outstanding book! Great ideas for anyone who wants to communicate better. I highly recommend it."

— *Nido R. Qubein*, CSP, CPAE

"If you are looking for a single-written source on the subject of effective presentations, Dr. Karen Lawson's new book, Involving Your Audience: Making It Active, *is for you. As a presentation skills coach, author, and communications specialist, I would highly recommend this comprehensive book as a gateway to knowledge on involving your audience."*

— *Patricia Ball*, CSP, CPAE, 1996–97 President of the National Speakers Association and author of *Straight Talk Is More Than Words*

"As an 'In Your Face,' audience-involving speaker myself, this book speaks my language. I firmly believe that if you involve your audiences, using techniques described by Karen Lawson in this book, they will learn more, laugh more, and appreciate you more."

— Tony Alessandra, PhD, CSP, CPAE, author of The Platinum Rule and Charisma

"Karen Lawson's book, Involving Your Audience: Making It Active, is a complete guide for anyone who wants to not just reach an audience but to really teach an audience.

Every speaker needs to read Involving Your Audience: Making It Active to insure maximum effectiveness and success on the platform. She has made a wonderful difference in my presentations."

Ralph Archbold, CSP, CPAE

"Wow, Karen Lawson has outdone herself in this new book on presentation skills. I read this and was inspired by all the unique insights. I am always looking to increase my skills and found Karen's book insightful. Congrats', Karen, on a job well done."

— Mikki Williams, CSP

"If you are looking for the best resource you can find to add interactive pizazz to your keynote or training session, look no further. Karen Lawson's book will provide you with more ideas than you can possibly use. Your biggest problem will be in deciding which are most helpful to you. Buy it; study it; use it; and don't lend it out."

— George Morrisey, CSP CPAE, author of Morrisey on Planning

INVOLVING YOUR AUDIENCE

Making It Active

KAREN LAWSON

WILLIAM D. THOMPSON
Series Editor

ALLYN AND BACON

Boston London Toronto Sydney Tokyo Singapore

**To my father, Byron Eells,
who taught me the power of words, and
to Professor Lyle Crist,
who taught me how to use them.**

Copyright © 1999 by Karen Lawson
Allyn and Bacon
A Viacom Company
160 Gould Street
Needham Heights, Massachusetts 02494

Internet: www.abacon.com

0-205-26811-0

Printed in the United States of America
10 9 8 7 6 5 4 3 2 1   02 01 00 99 98

Contents

Preface

The goal of every speaker is to connect with the audience, and one of the most effective ways of connecting with an audience is to get its members involved. Audience involvement can take several forms. You can involve your audience by using direct interaction, in which audience members are engaged in an activity with you or with each other. For example, you might have them discuss something with those seated close to them, or you might pose questions and solicit answers. You can also involve audience members by engaging them emotionally or mentally through storytelling and a variety of sensory-stimulating techniques. Through words, speakers create a virtual reality in which audience members almost become a part of the experience the speaker is describing.

Many speakers shy away from audience involvement for the following reasons:

1. Audience involvement takes time. Not only does it take time away from the speaker's actual delivery of the message, but also it takes time to plan how one will incorporate these techniques into the speech or presentation.
2. Audience involvement can be risky. Many speakers are afraid that they may lose control of the situation.
3. Audience involvement requires a different approach. Speakers sometimes prefer to stick to the tried-and-true method of simply standing before an audience and delivering their powerful messages. The ability to involve the audience in a more active way requires a different skill set that many speakers have not yet mastered. They may want to, but they don't know how. Besides, their traditional approach to speaking has brought them success for years, so they may see no need to change.

This last reason may be the most compelling force preventing speakers from trying a new approach. They simply see no need to do so. The most successful speakers, however, are those who are up-to-date on current trends. These trends apply not only to subject matter but also to audience needs and interests.

Programs must offer practical, how-to information, immediately applicable and transferable to the work, home, or school environment. Attendees also expect quality speakers and content-laden take-home materials.

Today's audiences are different from yesterday's. Conditioned by their experiences in school and corporate training programs, they expect to be involved. They expect a speech or a presentation to be a learning experience, and they expect a learning experience to be an active one. Furthermore, contemporary audiences are greatly influenced by computer games and simulations as well as by videos and television. With a multitude of television channels at their fingertips, people are less tolerant of limited programming options. They want to be wowed by both quality content and quality entertainment, and it's incumbent on us as speakers to deliver.

Today's speakers are knowledgeable and sophisticated, experts in their fields who can deliver compelling points and meaty content and who are dedicated to meeting the specific needs of audiences and meeting participants. Today's speakers are also entertaining. We know we face competition from videos, television, and multimedia productions. Speakers are concentrating more on audience involvement and interactive sessions.

Speakers are beginning to develop products such as tapes and books as ways to augment their presentations, generate additional income, and enhance their marketing efforts. Many are beginning to employ high-tech equipment, such as multiple screens, computer-generated graphics, and special effects. That translates into more pressure on everyone to remain competitive.

What does this all mean? It means greater opportunities to be a significant part of a growing and dynamic business, whether you are a beginner or a seasoned pro. It means more opportunities to establish partnerships and linkages between the meeting planner and speaker to better meet the client's needs.

With these points in mind, *Involving Your Audience: Make It Active* will provide professional speakers, trainers, consultants, Toastmasters, advanced university students, and others interested in public speaking with proven techniques that can be used to connect with audience members by actively involving them in the process. This book is a practical, how-to approach to using interactive methods to increase audience impact and ensure speaker success whether you are delivering a keynote speech, making a sales presentation, or conducting a seminar or training session.

The book is arranged in three parts. Part I focuses on helping you understand your audience, as well as yourself. Chapter 1 looks at audience demographics; Chapter 2 addresses both audience and speaker attitudes, value systems, and style differences; and Chapter 3 helps speakers gain a better understanding of audience needs and expectations.

Part II presents various ways of involving your audience visually. It includes a chapter on visual aids (Chapter 4); another chapter deals with the theatrical elements of speaking (Chapter 5); and a final chapter that addresses ways to create word pictures for your audience (Chapter 6).

Part III shows how to involve your audience through doing. Chapter 7 suggests ways to promote audience participation. Chapter 8 presents tips and techniques for interacting directly with your audience. Chapter 9 will help you handle that tricky, but so important, question-and-answer period. Finally, Chapter 10 offers strategies for handling as well as preventing difficult situations.

Professionals as well as students will benefit from this
book. Professionals will learn how to adapt existing material
to a more interactive delivery style. Students will learn how
to write and develop a speech from a perspective different
from the traditional approach in most academic settings.

ACKNOWLEDGMENTS

I express my appreciation to my friends and colleagues in the
National Speakers Association for their generosity and willingness to share their creative approaches to interactive speaking:
Ralph Archbold, Arden Bercovitz, Don Blohowiak, Marjorie
Brody, Carol Kivler, Mary Beth Roach, Bill Stieber, Glenna Salsbury, Suzy Sutton, and Mikki Williams. I am grateful to my
friend and colleague, Mel Silberman, from whom I learned
many of the audience involvement techniques cited in this
book. I am also grateful to Bill Thompson for inviting me to
be a part of *The Essence of Public Speaking Series.*

Finally, I thank Carol Hunsberger for her tireless proof-
reading and editing. As always, I express my gratitude to my
husband, Robert Lawson, and to my mother, Mildred Eells,
for their love and support.

Demographic Influences and Challenges

The first rule for any speaker is to know your audience. Not only will knowing all you can about the audience help you in tailoring your speech, presentation, or training session, but also it will help prevent disasters. This is particularly critical as our audiences become more diverse. An unfortunate episode illustrates this point. Several years ago, my partner was scheduled to conduct a training session on project management for a large international pharmaceutical company. The audience consisted of 12, fast-track, new management trainees from all over the world. The group was fairly evenly divided in terms of men versus women. The night before the session, my partner became quite ill, and despite all his efforts, he was even worse the next morning when I called at 6:00 A.M. Unfortunately, I was out of town getting ready to deliver another program to another client and so was unable to take over. I began making frantic phone calls to associates who I knew had some background in project management. I finally found someone who said she would rearrange her schedule and would be able to make it to the client's site by noon. I called the client to explain the situation, and she agreed to use my associate. Because the participants were in the United States for only a short period during which they were following a tight training schedule, there was little room for adjustment. I explained to our substitute trainer who the audience members were, why they were there, and what they would be doing with the information they would be learning in the session. I distinctly remember emphasizing that they were a multinational audience. When I called my client the next day to see how the session went, I was surprised when she told me that it had been a disaster. I couldn't imagine what could have gone wrong. After all, I wrote the program, and all the trainer had to do was to deliver it as written. Unfortunately, she chose to do her own thing. My client told me that the "Planning a Wedding" activity was a failure. I had no idea what she was talking about because I knew I had no such activity in my program. Apparently, the trainer had used the idea of how to plan a wedding as the example of how to plan and manage a project. Obviously, the topic was inappropriate for a mixed-gender audience and especially for a group in which there would be many cultural differences involved in planning a wedding. Clearly, the trainer had paid no attention to the demographic differences. As a result, not only was the session a disaster, but also we had to refund our fee and we lost the client.

There is no doubt about it—audiences have changed. To successfully connect with today's audiences, speakers must understand who they are and what they want or expect. To find out that information, you must do your homework. Furthermore, our diverse audiences require us to be sensitive to the broad spectrum of backgrounds and cultures of the people who attend our programs. Knowledge of the topics covered in this chapter is vital to every successful speaker.

AUDIENCE MAKEUP

Age

First, it is important to know the average age of the audience members. Why? Because different age groups have different needs and expectations. They also have different frames of reference. To be successful, you will need to adjust your style and use examples all participants can relate to. For example, references to television programs or music from the 1950s will have no meaning for those in their twenties or thirties. They will stare at you blankly if you start using examples from "Howdy Doody" or "Kukla, Fran, and Ollie." By the same token, those over fifty may have no idea what you're talking about if you mention "Beavis and Butt-head."

Gender

You will also want to know your audience's gender ratio. I would certainly not use gender-specific examples when talking to a mixed audience. Nor would I use hairdresser stories when speaking to a male-dominated group or sports analogies when addressing a room full of women. Aside from the fact that people in the audience might not be able to relate to the examples, there is a major risk of stereotyping, a dangerous practice in any situation.

Race, Ethnicity, Cultural Background

Information about cultural backgrounds can be helpful in shaping your speech or presentation. Once again, you will want to choose stories and examples audience members can relate to. This is particularly important when you are speaking to international audiences: stories that relate specifically to the American experience may be lost on them. Instead, concentrate on using stories that focus on the human experience, regardless of the country or cultural background.

For example, I once attended a concurrent session at an international training conference. The room was packed with 3,000 people, 25 percent of whom were from outside the United States. They had all come to learn from one of the training profession's gurus. The presenter started with a great technique to get people involved—the group sing-along. The only problem was that the song was about his hometown professional football team. At first glance, the audience *seemed* to be getting into the spirit of the activity. As I looked around the room, however, I noticed that about 25 percent of the participants (mostly our international guests) sat stone-faced, looking annoyed, confused, and certainly left out. Given the composition of the group, the presenter's choice of an audience involvement technique was somewhat questionable. But clearly, the subject highlighted in the activity (a U.S. football team) was highly inappropriate.

In addition to careful selection of anecdotes and other illustrations, you must also choose your words and expressions carefully. If you choose to use slang or idiomatic expressions, be sure to define them. Don't assume anything. If you refer to specific people as examples of a point you are trying to make, be sure these people are well known to everyone, or once again, explain who they are.

Religious Affiliation

Be very careful about discussing religion. Unless you are speaking to a group having a specific religious affiliation, be sure your points and illustrations include everyone. For example, during the December holidays, don't limit your references to Christmas, thereby assuming that everyone in the audience is Christian. Also mention Hanukkah and Kwaanza, for example. If the situation calls for some mention of attending a religious ceremony, be sure to mention synagogue, mosque, and temple as well as church.

Political Orientation

Politics can be just as volatile as religion. Be aware of, as well as respectful of, the fact that people of several political ideologies may be in your audience. Although comedians get laughs and applause by making political jokes, a professional should avoid demonstrating any type of bias. It's fine if you want to make a general reference to a political party or even a specific politician as long as it is done without disparagement.

Educational Background

You might also find it helpful to know something about the educational background of your audience members. You would certainly not refer to college experiences throughout your presentation if you knew that that the majority of your audience never attended college. Don't, however, assume that those with advanced degrees are any more intelligent than those with little or no formal education beyond high school. That erroneous assumption might influence you to talk down to a less-educated audience, resulting in your coming across as condescending and patronizing.

Economic Status

Knowledge of your audience's economic status will help you not only to choose appropriate stories and analogies but also to guide you in your choice of clothing. For example, if you are talking to a group of employees whose average salary is under $40,000, references to and examples of six-figure incomes and luxury purchases will probably alienate your audience. The key, once again, is to know how to relate to your audience.

Geographic Location

Keep in mind that what works in one part of the country (or part of the world) may not work in another. So always remember where you're speaking and where the audience members are from. This is an even more important consideration when speaking internationally. Take the time to learn about the area's history, important landmarks, and points of interest and be sure to include them in your presentation. If you don't speak the language, make an effort to learn the basics.

Several years ago, I went to Puerto Rico to do a two-day session for managers in a pharmaceutical company. I learned first-hand how important it is to be aware of cultural differences. I decided to go two days early to take advantage of the opportunity to relax on one of the beautiful beaches of San Juan. About midmorning, I returned to my room to retrieve something I had forgotten and noticed my message light blinking. When I checked my messages, I had a call from my client contact who asked me if I would be willing to go to the plant site a day earlier so the folks I would be working with there could meet me. Being the client-focused person that I am, I of course said yes, and the next morning, I was up at the crack of dawn and on my way to the plant. As I soon discovered, it was important to my Puerto Rican hosts that they have an opportunity to get to know me and to establish a relationship before I entered the classroom.

Using this experience as a cue, I decided to add a little human touch. Even though I don't speak a word of Spanish, I was determined to open and close my session with a few sentences in their language. So I wrote out my opening and closing in English and asked someone in human resources to translate it into Spanish for me. Then I got a little coaching on pronunciation, and I spent the evening memorizing my opening lines to welcome the participants to my workshop. Although I was a bit nervous, I managed to deliver my greeting without too many errors. But what I said or how I said it didn't matter. The participants were immensely pleased that I had made the effort to address them in their own language. I immediately had their cooperation and their respect because I had shown that I respected them.

Occupations/Positions

This piece of information is very important in helping you develop and deliver your speech, presentation, or program. I have seen several speakers fail miserably by assuming that people in the audience were managers. I have witnessed trainers who used assessment instruments and gave examples that would have meaning only for those who had people reporting to them.

Be careful not to let titles fool you. For example, let's assume you have been asked to deliver a speech or a seminar on time management for managers. Because you are dealing with a group of managers, you decide to devote a significant portion of your presentation to delegation techniques, failing to consider that a person having the title "manager" may manage projects, not people, and therefore, would have no one to whom he or she could delegate. Not only do you run the danger of "losing" those participants, but also you may alienate them if they are stressed by having a demanding work load and no one to help them out. That alienation could result in hostile behavior.

Parental Status

In today's world of blended families, extended families, and single-parent families, speakers must recognize and respect these lifestyle differences. We must be careful not to define families too narrowly when we refer to family experiences in our presentations. After all, a vast number of people in our audiences cannot identify with the "ideal" family portrayed in early television programs like "Ozzie and Harriet" or "Father Knows Best."

Knowledge of Subject

The amount of knowledge or degree of experience your audience members have with your topic is a significant piece of information. Once again, many a speaker has failed because he or she made an erroneous assumption either that the audience members knew more about the subject or that they knew less. If you assume that your audience members know much less than they really do, you risk insulting their intelligence or, at best, offering no new information, leaving them feeling that they have wasted their time. If you assume that they know more, you will probably be talking over their heads and they will leave feeling that something is missing.

Interests

If you know something about the interests or hobbies of the majority of your audience members, you will be able to use that information to create interesting scenarios, tell specific stories related to those interests, or use metaphors and analogies that they can relate to.

Disabilities

Knowing whether any participant or audience member has a disability is particularly important for the speaker who uses audience interaction. Some activities may have to be modified or eliminated. For example, I contracted to conduct a series of customer service training sessions throughout Pennsylvania for the people who operate the photo license centers. These centers are staffed by the Pennsylvania Industries for the Blind and Handicapped. I was aware of the special needs of some of the participants, such as those who were visually impaired or used wheelchairs, and made appropriate adjustments to my material and delivery methods. I was thrown a curve, however, when a young hearing-impaired woman attended my session without an interpreter. I did not discover this fact until I introduced an activity designed to illustrate the importance of active listening. It involves partic-

ipants closing their eyes, listening, and following my instructions. Obviously, this woman was unable to participate. I did
adjust my delivery, making sure I positioned myself so the
woman could read my lips and writing instructions and
important points on flipchart paper.

Size

Although not a demographic issue, the size of your audience
is an important factor in shaping your speech or presentation. You will choose your audio-visual support accordingly,
and you will also select activities and other interactions
depending on whether your group is small, medium, or large.
Many strategies can be used regardless of the number of people—only the logistics become a little more complicated. We
will explore some of those activities and strategies in Chapters 7 and 8.

Other Considerations

You will also want other information about your audience
members, such as why they are there, problems or concerns,
trends in the industry, attitude toward the subject, likes and
dislikes, organization(s) represented, and subjects to avoid.
We will address the specifics of these factors in Chapters 2
and 3.

   At this point, you may be asking yourself, "Where or how
do I get this information?" The answer is simple: from the
meeting planner or your client contact. You can also find out
some information about the organization or industry by reading an organization's annual report or the industry's trade
publications or by surfing the Net. Much information is readily available through free Internet information services that
offer up-to-the-minute information 24 hours a day, including
news stories and business and industry updates. To obtain

specific information about the audience, I recommend developing a questionnaire like the one used by Suzy Sutton (see Figure 1.1 on the next 3 pages) to send to the meeting planner to fill out, or you can use it to capture the information during a telephone or face-to-face interview. In any case, the important thing is to do your homework.

While it is true that having this wealth of information will help prepare you to meet your audience's needs, be sure to exercise caution. Because you have so much information, you might easily find yourself falling into the stereotype trap. You make the assumption, for example, that a group of accountants will be serious and stuffy. Because of your assumption, you may decide to focus on presenting straightforward, somewhat dry information, afraid that accountants wouldn't enjoy or appreciate interactive activities. Nothing could be further from the truth. In fact, one of my most lively and creative training audiences was a group of accountants from one of the large accounting firms.

Although you will want to gather specific information about your audience each time you present, it might be helpful to review some information about today's audiences in general. The Hudson Institute's Workforce 2000 study tells us that by the year 2000, 85 percent of those entering the work force will be women, members of minority groups, and immigrants. In addition, there will be more physically and mentally challenged workers as well as more older workers as the "baby boomers" turn fifty. In 1985, white males made up 47 percent of the labor force, whereas only 15 percent of the new workers entering the workplace were white males. Not only can organizations not conduct business as usual, but also speakers cannot afford to ignore this changing landscape. The implications for us as speakers is that we can be a driving force in recognizing the opportunities that a diverse environment and work force offer and that we can take advantage of the ideas, creativity, and assets of a multicultural population.

Figure 1.1

Program Questionnaire

YOUR NAME
ORGANIZATION
ADDRESS

Organization _____

Scheduled date(s) _____ Time _____

Location _____ Length _____

Topic _____ Estimated attendance _____

Contact person/Coordinator _____

Phone number _____ E-mail address _____

My goal is to tailor my program to meet the specific needs of your group. This questionnaire will help me prepare that program. Please answer all the questions as fully as possible. Feel free to skip any questions which are irrelevant for this program.

Please return this form to my office no later than _____ along with any additional information you feel would help me understand your organization (brochures, newsletters, etc.).

Thank you! Your valuable input will increase the value of my program to your group.

1. What is the purpose of the meeting? Is there a theme? _____
    _____
    _____
    _____

2. What are your specific objectives for my session? _____
    _____
    _____
    _____

3. Are there any particular issues/topics that you would like me to address during the program? _____
    _____
    _____
    _____

4. Are there any sensitive issues to avoid? _____
    _____

5. Name/title of my introducer: _____

6. What takes place immediately before my program? _____
    _____

7. Entire meeting:

   Date _____ Starting time _____

   Date _____ Ending time _____

8. My program:

   Date _____ Starting time _____

   Date _____ Ending time _____

9. What takes place immediately after my program? _____
   _____
   _____

10. Who are the other speakers on the program (if any)?

    Speaker _____ Topic _____

    Speaker _____ Topic _____

11. What professional speakers have you used in the past and what did they cover?

    Speaker _____ Topic _____

    Speaker _____ Topic _____

12. Please provide me with the names/titles/phone numbers of two people who will be at my presentation. I might call them to do more "grass-roots" information gathering.

    a. _____
    _____

    b. _____
    _____

13. AUDIENCE PROFILE:

    Percentage of males? _____ Percentage of females? _____

    Average age of group? _____ Range of age: _____ to _____

    Educational background _____
    _____

    Occupations _____
    _____

    Cultural backgrounds _____

    Socioeconomic status _____

    Other (if applicable) _____

    Religious affiliation _____

Political orientation _____

Primary language _____

14. What are the top challenges/concerns faced by participants? _____

_____

_____

15. What have been the most significant events in your industry, group, or organization during the last year? (e.g., mergers, trends, relocations, new technology, etc.) _____

_____

_____

_____

16. Are there any "buzz words" or technical terms to be aware of? _____

_____

_____

17. Any other suggestions to help make this program the best ever? _____

_____

_____

LOGISTICAL INFORMATION:

18. How do I get to the meeting site/hotel? _____

_____

_____

_____

19. Name and phone number of contact person at hotel in case I have any problems/emergencies on the way. _____

_____

_____

2 Audience and Speaker Attitudes, Value Systems, and Style Differences

In addition to the obvious demographic considerations we discussed in Chapter 1, we must also take into consideration audience attitudes, value systems, and style differences. These considerations have a major impact on the speaker's choice of interactive delivery methods.

ATTITUDES

Today's audiences, characterized as demanding, sophisticated, and skeptical, require a different approach in order to connect with them. Some people in our audiences believe that they have heard it all before and have adopted a jaded, "show-me-how-you're-different" attitude. What will set the really good speakers apart from the mediocre ones is their ability to position or deliver their message with a different spin.

WANTING A QUICK FIX

Other audience members come with the mindset reflective of our quick-fix, "I-want-it-all-and-I-want-it-now" society. In fact, some new speakers share a similar attitude. I often receive phone calls from aspiring speakers who want some information and guidance on how to break into the speaking or training profession. I generally suggest one or more of the following basic strategies:

- Volunteer to speak for free to various civic and professional groups to gain name recognition, credibility, and experience.
- Read books about speaking to understand better the profession and the mechanics of speaking.
- Listen to tapes of well-known speakers to pick up pointers on delivery style and delivery techniques.
- Attend presentation skills or train-the-trainer classes to fine-tune your skills.
- Join Toastmasters International and the local chapter of the National Speakers Association (NSA) to network with others in the profession, to increase your knowledge of speaking and the speaking business, and to sharpen skills.

I'm always amazed by the reaction of many novices, who dismiss my suggestions. Some tell me they don't have time to do all those things. Others say they don't need to attend any classes because they are already good at speaking in front of groups. Still others take the position that they want to be regarded as professionals and that they therefore have no intention of speaking for free.

ENTITLEMENT

Another attitudinal issue is that of entitlement. You may find that people use a "you-owe-me" attitude to justify behaviors such as padding expense reports, making personal calls from work, using the office copier for personal projects, or helping themselves to office supplies. These attitudes play an important role in how people in our audiences perceive us. Attitudes are also reflected in audience members' behaviors, which can either support or undermine a speaker's efforts. For instance, I was conducting an all-day session on managing conflict. The session was based almost entirely on real-life, organization-specific case studies I had developed based on interactions in interviews and focus groups. One case always presents a challenge. I put people into groups to analyze the case and determine which conflict management approach and strategy would be the most appropriate. This is the case's scenario:

> You have been asked by the executive vice president to work on a special project. To complete this project, you need information from one of the vice presidents in another area of the organization. You have asked her for the information, but she dismisses you every time by telling you she is too busy and will get to it as soon as she can. Out of frustration, you go to your manager and ask him to intervene. He promises to talk with the vice president but, so far, he has not. The deadline is near, and you still don't have the information. And the situation doesn't look very encouraging. What should you do?

In one session, one group came up with an interesting response. Their suggested approach was to go to the vice president (VP) one more time, and if she didn't cooperate, to invoke the name of the executive vice president (EVP) and the veiled threat that they would tell him that she was uncooperative. I suggested in our full-class discussion that they might consider possible consequences of that action. To them, it was quite simple. If they threatened the VP, they were sure she would cave in, and their problem would be solved. I tried to get them to think about possible repercussions down the road, but they could think of none. When I finally offered the possibility that the VP might give them what they wanted but that this approach could come back to haunt them, they told me that they only cared about impressing the EVP and that they didn't care at all about the VP's reaction to them. They could not see any way that the VP could impact their careers. Furthermore, they informed me that they were on a fast track and that they weren't going to let someone like her get in their way. It was quite an interesting and enlightening discussion.

VALUES

Today's audiences represent an interesting mix of values. Some people primarily value their home and family lives; others their careers. Some value loyalty to their companies, others to their professions, and still others to themselves. Some value money, while others are more concerned with security.

Values are the underpinnings and the basis for understanding ourselves and others. Values are the degree of importance one places on something; values provide the basis for our ethical behavior.

Your own values play a big part in the way you relate to or interact with an audience. You are sometimes expected to say or do something that is contrary to your belief system. When that happens, you have several choices: you can either go along with your client's wishes, stick by your convictions and express yourself honestly in front of the group, or turn down the engagement. First and foremost, you must be true to yourself. There must be congruence between what you say and what you do and that congruence must come across to the audience.

A number of years ago, I attended a training session conducted by one of the gurus of the training profession. I had heard so much about him, and I was thrilled that he was finally coming to our city. Right before and during the training session, he was Mr. Personality Plus. He was warm, sincere, and engaging. When the session ended, I approached him to tell him how much I enjoyed the program. Contrary to his platform persona, he was cold and aloof, he avoided eye contact, and he acted as though I was imposing. I also observed that he exhibited similar behavior to others. The incongruity between his on-stage and his off-stage behavior left a negative impression that I have never forgotten.

Clarifying Your Values

To understand our audiences, we need to understand ourselves first. A good starting place is to clarify our own values.

Let's start by taking a look at where our values come from. Our values are shaped by our environment and the people around us—first our parents, then our teachers and school environment, our friends, and our religious affiliation. The media, the culture and geographic region in which we live, historical events taking place around us, and our own individual significant emotional events all play a role in creating our value systems.

The time in which we live has a profound impact. Dr. Morris Massey, well known for his work in the area of value programming, asserts that we are products of our environment. In his 1976 videotape presentation *What You Are Is Where You Were Then*, Dr. Massey tells us that our values, formed by our surroundings, are established by age 10 and locked in by age 20. Our values can be altered, however, by what Dr. Massey calls a significant emotional event.

A significant emotional event is an event or experience, positive or negative, immediate or cumulative, that has a profound impact on us. The death of a loved one, a divorce, or losing one's job are examples of immediate significant emotional events. Parenting is an example of a significant emotional event that is cumulative. In any case, such events result in providing us with powerful insight that ultimately leads to a change or shift in our values.

Although our values help define who we are and influence what we do, many of us have never had the opportunity to think about and examine closely what we value and why. To gain additional personal insight, use the following self-assessment to explore what's really important to you.

Values Clarification Activity

Instructions: For each of the following values, indicate their degree of importance to you using the following scale:

1 = Extremely important

2 = Quite important

3 = Moderately important

4 = Unimportant

Then look at those you have chosen as extremely important and put a star or asterisk by your top three choices.

_____ **Knowledge and Wisdom**
To learn new things and ideas; personal growth through experience.

_____ **Morality and Ethics**
To maintain a sense of right and wrong; to adhere to socially accepted standards.

_____ **Freedom and Independence**
To be able to make your own decisions and use your own judgment.

_____ **Love and Affection**
To experience a sense of caring for and from other people.

Money and Security
To have enough income and resources to provide for wants and needs; to feel safe in your environment.

Mental and Physical Health
To be free of stress, anxiety, and physical illness; to be fit and energetic.

Religious and Spiritual Beliefs
To believe in a Supreme Being or spiritual force.

Friendship
To have a sense of belonging to a person or group; companionship.

Pleasure
To participate in things you like to do; to have fun and enjoy life.

Achievement and Accomplishment
To have a feeling of self-satisfaction as a result of completing a task, overcoming an obstacle, or meeting a challenge.

Loyalty and Trust
To experience a feeling of dedication and commitment to friends, family, country, organization, and so on; to have confidence in the integrity and honesty of others.

Power and Influence
To have a sense of control and influence over yourself and others.

Justice
To believe in a system that rewards positive behavior and punishes negative; sense of fairness.

Recognition
To receive praise and rewards for accomplishments and contributions.

After you have reviewed your values, think about how they influence you and your behavior and interactions with others. How do your values impact your audience? How do others' values impact you? Do you react when a participant's values differ dramatically from yours? How are your values reflected in your speaking? By focusing on your own set of values, you can better understand yourself and your audience.

PERCEPTUAL MODALITIES

An effective speaker or trainer needs to be cognizant of the many "perceptual modalities" represented by our audience members. According to M. B. James and M. W. Galbraith, a learner may prefer one of the following six "perceptual modalities"; that is, ways in which one takes in and processes information (James and Galbraith, 1985):

Visual   Videos, slides, graphs, photos, demonstrations, exhibits
Print   Texts, paper-and-pencil exercises
Aural   Lectures, audio tapes
Interactive   Group discussions, question-and-answer sessions
Tactile   Hands-on activities, model building
Kinesthetic   Role plays, physical games, and activities

The challenge to speakers and trainers is to make sure our presentations address each of these modalities to some degree. If we use the interactive techniques addressed throughout this book, this shouldn't be a problem.

STYLE DIFFERENCES

An often-overlooked source of conflict and misunderstanding between people is personality, behavior, and communication styles. There are many assessment instruments on the market, including the *Myers-Briggs Type Indicator (MBTI)*, published by Consulting Psychologists Press; the *Life Orientations Survey (LIFO)*, by Stuart Atkins; the *Personal Profile System*, by Carlson Learning; the *Style Analysis*, by Target Training International; *What's My Style?* by HRDQ; *Behavioral Profiles*, developed by Tony Alessandra and published by Jossey-Bass/Pfeiffer; and *I Speak Your Language*, by Drake Beam Morin, to name a few. The purpose of these instruments is to provide you with insight into your style as well as into others' styles in order to improve interpersonal effectiveness. Most are based on personality theory put forth by Carl Jung in the early 1900s. Jung identified "psychological types" based on patterns of behavior. According to Jung, people follow certain behavior patterns in the way they prefer to perceive and make judgments.

Over the years, theorists and practitioners have modified, expanded, and applied Jung's theory to the development of their own instruments. If you have not yet done so, I highly recommend that you complete a self-assessment instrument such as those listed above. It is a useful tool in the effort to expand your self-awareness and to grow as a speaker and as a person. It will help you to understand yourself and those who attend your programs better. Your awareness of these style differences will help you to reach and interact with your audience members more effectively.

To get a flavor of these style differences, read each of the following statements and circle the ending that is most like you.

1. When I am in a learning situation, I like to . . .
   a. be involved in doing something.
   b. work with people in groups.
   c. read about the information.
   d. watch and listen to what is going on.

2. When I am working in a group, I like to . . .
   a. direct the discussion and activity.
   b. find out what other people think and feel.
   c. remain somewhat detached from the rest of the group.
   d. go along with the majority.

3. When faced with a conflict situation, I prefer to . . .
   a. confront the situation head on and try to win.
   b. work with the other person to arrive at an amicable resolution.
   c. present my position by using logic and reason.
   d. not make waves.

4. In a conversation, I tend to . . .
   a. come straight to the point.
   b. draw others into the conversation.
   c. listen to what others have to say then offer an objective opinion.
   d. agree with what others say.

5. When making a decision, I tend to . . .
   a. make a decision quickly and then move on.
   b. consider how the outcome will affect others.
   c. take time to gather facts and data.
   d. consider all possible outcomes and proceed with caution.

6. I am seen by others as someone who . . .
   a. gets results.
   b. is fun to be with.
   c. is logical and rational.
   d. is a calming influence.

7. In a work environment, I prefer . . .
   a. to work alone.
   b. to work with others.
   c. structure and organization.
   d. a peaceful atmosphere.

Now count the number of items circled for each letter. The letter with the most circles indicates your preferred style:

a   =   Candid

b   =   Persuasive

c   =   Logical

d   =   Reflective

As you read the brief descriptions below, determine for yourself the accuracy of the description as it reflects your personal style.

Candid

Candid individuals are direct and controlling. They like to be in charge and the center of attention. They are action-oriented and may be perceived as pushy and domineering. They enjoy being challenged, and they tend to make decisions quickly, sometimes with little information. Those having a candid style are demanding of themselves and others.

To be more effective, the candid person needs to be more sensitive to others, to practice active listening, and to exercise more caution in making decisions. If you are a speaker who has this primary style, you might need to be more patient with those who take longer to ask or answer a question. You would benefit from taking the time to make sure you really heard what an audience member said before responding. Another behavior to monitor is the tendency to show impatience by interrupting or displaying negative facial expressions.

Persuasive

Those individuals whose primary style is persuasive love people. They are outgoing, warm, and animated. They are very sociable and may be perceived as overly emotional. They have a short attention span and dislike details. Persuasive individuals are spontaneous, entertaining, and like to take risks.

To be more effective, the persuasive person needs to improve organization skills and spend more time looking at the facts. The speaker who has a persuasive personality orientation may need to guard against becoming too casual or familiar with certain audiences. Another potential danger might be the tendency to be too open and self-disclosing. To guard against being perceived as unorganized, be sure to have appropriate data to back up your points or assertions.

Logical

Logical individuals pride themselves on their use of analysis and reason in all situations. They have a strong need to be right, and they rely on facts and data to support their positions. Although they are good problem solvers, they are slow to make decisions. They are sometimes perceived as aloof and critical. They often ask probing questions and frequently take the opposite point of view in a discussion.

To be more effective, the logical person should learn to be more flexible, to spend less time gathering data, to show more concern for people, and to be more expressive of his or her feelings. If you have this style, you would benefit from using more personal stories and from building more humor into your presentations. You might also try focusing less on content and more on the emotional needs of the audience.

Reflective

Reflective individuals are reliable and cautious. They tend to be perfectionists and to seek security. They avoid conflict and may be perceived by others as weak. Reflective people are good listeners and make great friends. They are loyal, cooperative, and supportive. For this reason, they are good team players.

To be more effective, the reflective person should learn to be more assertive, less sensitive, and more willing to take risks. A speaker who is reflective might consider taking more risks by trying new techniques, such as adding music and using more audience participation.

While it's true that speakers must be true to themselves and adopt their own style, our ability and willingness to be flexible and to try new things will help us grow as speakers. By understanding style differences and by learning to accept and adjust to those differences, we can be more effective in our relationships with our audiences. Not only can we influence others through our ability to adjust our styles to theirs, but also our acceptance of them and our willingness to adapt influences others to accept and adapt to us as well.

3 Audience Needs and Expectations

As mentioned earlier, today's audiences are demanding and have short attention spans. They want it all. They want to be entertained as well as to receive practical information and high-quality delivery.

To understand today's audiences, first we must understand what motivates them. We can analyze audiences by taking a simple look at them in relation to Maslow's hierarchy of needs. Maslow's theory identifies five levels of need: physiological, safety/security, social/belonging, recognition/status, and self-actualization.

UNDERSTANDING BASIC HUMAN NEEDS

Physiological

In the true sense of the term, *physiological needs* refer to food, clothing, and shelter. As the term relates to our audiences, these needs refer to the basic physical comfort of audience members created by the appropriate room temperature, comfortable chairs, proper lighting, the sound system, and freedom of movement. Once these needs have been met, audience members will be physically receptive to listening to our messages.

Safety/Security

The next level of audience needs is concerned with members' safety needs. According to Maslow, people have two sets of needs—one set that strives for growth and one set that clings to safety—important components in creating an environment that meets audience members' emotional needs. Creating a safe environment is particularly important in interactive speaking. You must create a climate of trust if you expect the audience to interact with you or even with each other. Unless the audience mambers trust you, they will resist any attempts to get them directly involved in the speech, presentation, or seminar. Once that trust factor has been established, audiences will do almost anything you ask.

Social/Belonging

People are by nature social beings. With this in mind, you can really capitalize on this level of need. People want to interact with others in situations where they feel they belong and are accepted. Interactive speaking enables people to interact with each other in pairs or small groups. This social element further enhances the audience's receptivity to a speaker's message because they are enjoying the experience and sharing it with others.

This need for sharing became quite clear to me several years ago in New York. When the *Phantom of the Opera* opened on Broadway, I was ecstatic and couldn't wait to see it. As luck would have it, I was scheduled to present at a training conference shortly after the play opened, so I quickly ordered my ticket for an evening performance. Unfortunately, I had to go by myself because my husband was unable to join me and my colleagues had other plans. I was so excited! I had waited for months for this opportunity. So on the night of the performance, I donned my best evening attire, hired a limousine, and went to the theater—alone. The play exceeded my expectations. The music, the staging, the acting were fabulous. Although I enjoyed the play itself, I found myself getting more and more depressed as the evening wore on, particularly when I returned to my hotel. I stopped in the lobby lounge for a nightcap and began reflecting on my wonderful experience and wondering why I felt so empty. Then it dawned on me: I had no one to share the experience with. Hundreds and hundreds of people surrounded me, yet I was alone—just like many people in our audiences. You can prevent that feeling of loneliness by meeting the social need through interactive speaking techniques.

Recognition/Status

Most people tend to associate this level of need with an individual's need for prestige and power. Audience members who have this need will find fulfillment through opportunities to share the stage with the speaker, to take a leading role in a discussion group, or to respond to the speaker's questions. Other ways to meet this need are to mention people by name and to both recognize and reward people for their contributions. We will look at these techniques in later chapters. Another aspect of the recognition/status need, often overlooked, is the need for respect. The audience needs to feel that you respect them. You can demonstrate respect for audience members by not talking down to or insulting them, by acknowledging their knowledge and experience, by giving them an opportunity to share that experience, and by starting and ending on time.

Self-Actualization

Self-actualization is concerned primarily with personal achievement and esteem needs. You can address these needs by making audience members feel good about themselves. I have heard some speakers preach and moralize by telling their audiences what they "should do." Audience members may leave these presentations feeling dejected or angry. Good speakers, on the other hand, help people to recognize the beauty and goodness within themselves. Finally, they *invite* audience members to take action, not tell them what they must do. Effective speakers influence their audience members to be the best they can be by increasing their self-awareness and by helping them discover and uncover important life lessons and universal truths.

FINDING OUT ABOUT YOUR AUDIENCE

To meet specific needs, it's important to find out as much as you can about your audience well in advance of preparing your speech, presentation, or seminar. That way you can truly customize it or at least tailor it to the organization or industry. Some speakers confuse the words *tailor* and *customize*. When you *tailor* a speech or seminar, you are taking an existing presentation and adapting it to your audience by using industry-specific terminology and examples related to the audience's industry or organization. On the other hand, when you *customize* your program, you are developing it according to your client's specifications. Nothing is worse than listening to a speaker use examples that the audience can in no way relate to. For example, if I am addressing a group of new hires right out of college, it would not be appropriate for me to use examples or activities that pertain only to managers or senior executives.

Presession Questionnaire

Whenever possible, it's a good idea to send out a presession questionnaire to participants, particularly for programs that are six hours long or longer. The purpose of the questionnaire

Figure 3.1

Sample Presession Questionnaire

"Dealing with Conflict"

The purpose of this questionnaire is to provide the presenter of this program with insights into your current skills in or knowledge about the subject. By knowing what new skills and knowledge you would like to gain from the program, the presenter will be better able to meet your needs.

Name _____

Department _____ Position _____

Briefly describe the responsibilities of your position. _____
_____

How long have you been in this position? _____

Describe a conflict situation that currently exists or has happened recently in your department or work unit. _____
_____

How does this conflict affect working relationships? _____
_____

How does this conflict affect productivity? _____
_____

What would you like to learn about dealing with conflict? _____
_____

How do you expect this seminar will help you? _____
_____

is to uncover needs and expectations so that you can tailor your session to meet them. Figure 3.1 is a questionnaire for a program on managing conflict. Not only is it used to uncover specific concerns, but also it provides valuable information that can be used to create role plays, case studies, and other activities directly relevant to the participants' environment.

You might be thinking, "Well, this is great for a program for 25 or 30 people, but what about large audiences? I can't possibly send out questionnaires to 800 people." You may not be able or willing to survey hundreds of audience members, but you could mail to a random sampling.

Individual Participant Interviews and Focus Groups

It's also a good idea to interview a few participants before the speech or session to get a better feel for what they need and want. You can conduct these interviews with individuals one-on-one, face-to-face or by telephone. You can also meet with several people at once in focus groups. You might find that what you were told they need is totally off the mark.

Talk to the Meeting Planner

Don't overlook your partner in this process—the meeting planner. This person can provide valuable insight into the makeup of the group, the climate of the organization, the hidden needs, and other important background information. Be sure to ask the meeting planner about the percentage mix of content, entertainment, and interaction that is appropriate for the group. You should have this informal discussion even though you may be using a questionnaire like the one in Chapter 1 (see pages 11–13). Meeting planners are often willing to share information with you off the record that they will not put in writing. Be sure to ask what activities and interactive methods the group has already experienced or been exposed to through other speakers or training opportunities. A critical piece of several of my sessions is some type of personality assessment instrument. I always ask if the participants have had any exposure to self-assessment instruments and, if so, which ones. I can then choose something else.

We can't always plan, however, on getting accurate information from the meeting planner. The training director of a large chemical company asked me to do a stress management program for their executive secretaries. I asked him a number of questions, including what had prompted this request. Apparently, there had been a recent companywide meeting during which a large number of secretaries spoke out quite candidly about their dissatisfaction with the way things were being done. Senior management was quite alarmed by the secretaries' reaction and concluded that they needed stress management. To customize the program to their specific situation and needs, I suggested that I meet with a representative sample of the target population in a focus group setting. For two hours, I listened as these women voiced their frustrations. When the session was over, I met with the training director and told him I would be happy to conduct a stress management session if that's what he really wanted. But I added quite strongly that I didn't think it would do one bit of good. What they needed was communication and interpersonal skills training for both the secretaries and their managers. Fortunately, he took my advice and we delivered a very successful program entitled "The Boss–Secretary Relationship." If I had relied on only the input from the training director and not conducted the focus group session, the program would have been a miserable failure.

In addition to gathering information about the audience beforehand via questionnaires, telephone calls or interviews with participants, and discussions with the meeting planner, do a little reconnaissance on your own in person an hour or so before your presentation. Arrive early so you can mix and mingle and really get to know your audience on an individual basis. A social hour or any other structured networking activity prior to the formal program is a perfect opportunity. This rapport building will go a long way to prevent or defuse any hostility that could surface during your presentation. It's much more difficult to be antagonistic toward someone with whom you have connected personally. It is also a great way to identify specific people to use when personalizing examples or to enlist volunteers to participate in specific activities that we will discuss in Chapter 8. This one-on-one personal contact helps people see you as a real person, relaxed and approachable, not as some standoffish, arrogant prima donna.

Be sure to stick around after your presentation, also. It will give you the opportunity to reinforce your message, and it helps create a more favorable impression. Those who speak and run are often viewed as people interested only in doing a job and getting paid rather than as true professionals who care about people.

FOCUS ON THEIR NEEDS, NOT YOURS

Some speakers are so focused on impressing the audience with their knowledge, expertise, or style that they lose sight of why they were hired. The speaker's job is to meet audience members' needs whether they are psychological, emotional, spiritual, or intellectual. At the same time, we, as speakers, should attend to their physical needs as appropriate. As you recall, we addressed these earlier.

If you remember two important phrases, you will have no trouble focusing on audience needs. The first is WIIFM (What's In It For Me). Every person has a WIIFM. By showing audience members how your message or points are relevant to them, you will win their admiration and appreciation with no problem. Even more important, show how they can use your information to make their lives easier or more enjoyable or to enhance their own feelings of personal well-being.

The second guiding phrase is MMFI (Make Me Feel Important). This, of course, relates to the esteem need in Maslow's hierarchy, mentioned at the beginning of this chapter.

When you genuinely care about your audience, it shows. The platform has no place for supreme egos. We all have egos, particularly those of us in the speaking profession. If we didn't, we probably couldn't do what we do—risking public humiliation and rejection. But when we focus on our own egos, we lose that magical quality that bonds speaker and audience.

I was reminded of how important it is to put the ego aside by watching a colleague and friend present several years ago. She was a terrific presenter, and I really admired the way she captured and held an audience spellbound no matter how long the session. Her sessions were always interesting and included lots of audience participation. People could count on leaving with many helpful and practical how-tos as well as a positive, upbeat feeling about the experience. On this particular occasion, my friend decided to try a different approach. Instead of her usual audience-centered, highly interactive, content-rich presentation, she focused on the entertainment factor. Unfortunately, she went overboard. She sang, she danced, she told jokes, and she pulled out prop after prop and gimmick after gimmick. I was both sad and embarrassed for her as audience members got up and left, at first one by one and then in groups. Of course, she was devastated. She asked me to give her honest feedback about what she did wrong. So I told her bluntly, but kindly, to go back to doing what she does best: focusing on giving the audience members valuable information and techniques that help them do their jobs better. Every time I'm tempted to be something I'm not, I remember and heed my own words of wisdom.

A friend and colleague, Carol Kivler, has a great activity she uses to help people put their egos aside in her training sessions. At each participant's seat, Carol places a brown bag marked with his or her name. She tells the group up front that before they can be open to new ideas and new techniques, they have to put their egos away. She then asks them to open their bags, put their egos inside, and then tie the bags and put them in a box at the front of the room. In working with a group of college professors, she even had one person admit jokingly that his ego was too big to fit in the bag. That's a great symbolic lesson for all of us. We should probably all carry "ego bags" with us to every speaking engagement and remember to stuff our egos in the bag before we walk onto the stage or enter a training room.

SPEAKING TO DIFFERENT AGE GROUPS

The key to connecting with various age groups differs considerably. For example, people born between roughly 1943 and 1960 have been influenced by the events of the 1960s and 1970s. Idealistic and moralistic, the baby boomers' primary motivators have been money and freedom. Those born from 1920 to 1942 were impacted by the Great Depression and believe strongly in the importance of security and loyalty. Finally, people born between 1961 and 1979, the so-called Generation Xers, have grown up on computers, video games, and VCRs and are both realistic and cynical. They have grown up watching their workaholic parents spend 14 to 16 hours a day at the office, foregoing family vacations, only to find themselves tossed out after 25 years of loyal service to the company. Forget loyalty. Generation Xers want what they want now. They're interested in rewarding challenges and are willing to work hard. Yet unlike their parents, they fiercely guard their personal and leisure time. Because many grew up in dual-career or single-parent families, they are self-reliant and independent and are not as intimidated by authority figures as are those in previous generations. Consequently, they are not likely to take what we as speakers say because we are older, more experienced, or simply "in charge" of the seminar room or platform. Generation Xers will readily challenge our statements, and we had better be ready to deal with those challenges. With those audience members, we have to earn our credibility.

4 Using Visuals—Low Cost to High Tech

Every day of our lives, a barrage of visual images bombards us through both electronic and print media. Why? Because visual communication has the greatest impact on learning and retention. Although human beings process information through a variety and combination of perceptual modalities, studies show that more adults belong to the category of visual learners than to that of any other perceptual style.

There's no doubt about it—visuals are an important way to involve your audience. For years, speakers have been using visuals in various forms to increase their impact on their audiences.

RETENTION RATE IN VISUAL LEARNING

Visuals play an important role in helping audience members retain information. Research shows that people can retain only zero to five pieces of information. That means that we as speakers must find various ways to increase that retention rate.

Before we explore other reasons for using visual aids and specific examples, let's take a look at the research supporting their use. During the 1980s, the 3M Company sponsored two studies, one with the Wharton School's Applied Research Center and one with the University of Minnesota's Management Information Systems Research Center, to look at the impact of visuals (primarily overhead and computer-generated visuals) on business presentations and meetings. The results of these studies support the widely held belief that visuals do indeed increase retention and effectiveness. In fact, several studies have shown that people are primarily visual learners. It has been estimated that over 80 percent of all learning begins through the eyes.

The Wharton study (Oppenheim, 1981) found that presenters using overhead transparencies were perceived as significantly better prepared, more professional, more persuasive, more highly credible, and more interesting. Results from the University of Minnesota study (Vogel et al., 1996) show that when visuals are added to an oral presentation, retention is increased by about 10 percent and the presentation became more than 43 percent more persuasive. Furthermore, presenters using computer-generated visuals were perceived as being more concise, more professional, clearer, more persuasive, more interesting, and more effective in the use of supporting data.

Other Significant Findings

Both Harvard and Columbia conducted studies that had results similar to those of the studies conducted by Wharton and the University of Minnesota. Even more dramatic results are reflected in Edgar Dale's findings. His conclusions, now known as "Dale's Cone of Experience," show that people will remember (Walters, 1993):

- 20 percent of what they hear
- 30 percent of what they see
- 50 percent of what they see and hear
- 80 percent of what they hear, see, and do

The last conclusion provides additional support for the importance of involving your audience. If audience members have an opportunity actually to *do,* that is, participate, they will be more likely to remember your message.

WHY USE VISUAL AIDS?

The main purpose of visual aids is to enhance your speech or presentation and to improve retention. The key word here is *aid.* Visuals should not take the place of your spoken word. After all, if the visual can stand alone, the speaker is not necessary. I have seen presentations in which the speaker's entire presentation was dependent on the visual aid. For example, on one occasion, the speaker had prepared a glitzy and very expensive slide show. Her entire presentation was designed to be one slide after another, and her role was that of a talking head, who for the most part, advanced the slides and read from them. About a third of the way through the presentation, the electricity went off, and the speaker was totally unprepared to continue without her visual aids. She fumbled her way for the next few minutes and then was forced to end her presentation because she had nothing to say.

BENEFITS OF USING PRESENTATION MEDIA

The use of presentation media benefits both the presenter and the audience. Visuals help guide the audience and often make it easier for audience members to understand the speaker's message.

Media provide organization, which speeds comprehension. The following reasons for using visual aids form the acronym AROUSE: Attention, Reinforcement, Organization, Understanding, Support, and Emphasis. The word *arouse* means to stimulate or to elicit a strong response, a primary objective of every speaker.

Attention

Visual aids help get and keep the audience's attention. The visual aid can be extremely simple and even somewhat primitive, or it can be slick and dramatic. It all depends on factors such as personal choice, cost, available resources, type of presentation, room size and setup, audience, and your purpose. For example, I learned (quite by accident) about the powerful attention-getting impact of a simple visual many years ago when I was a high school English teacher. I was part of a three-person team teaching American Literature to high school juniors. We were in a large-group, small-group approach, which meant that two days a week, one of us lectured to all our combined classes at the same time. Imagine 150 16-year-olds in a lecture hall. Talk about a challenging audience! This was my first experience lecturing to a large group of teenagers, and my topic was Nathaniel Hawthorne and *The Scarlet Letter*. I knew this was not exactly a hot topic for a group of 16-year-olds. Furthermore, having observed the behavior of the group when the other two teachers lectured, I was petrified and knew that I needed to come up with some way to get the students' attention fast. I decided to take a transparency and buy a stencil of an Old English style letter *A*. I traced it on the transparency and colored it red by hand. (These were the days before computers and color printers.) I arrived at the lecture hall 20 minutes early and put the transparency on the overhead. I then dimmed the lights so that the students could just see where they were going. When the bell rang and the students came rushing and screaming into the lecture room, they stepped through the door and immediately became very quiet because all they could see was a huge, red *A* on the screen in a darkened room. They began taking their seats with hushed exchanges such as "Cool," "Heavy, man," "Far out," and so forth. (This was the 1970s.) I had their attention immediately and, as a result, I was able to conduct my lecture without the usual antics and disruptions the other teachers had experienced.

Reinforcement

Visual aids also reinforce the points you are making. With key words or graphics, the message is communicated both visually and verbally. As we noted earlier, the likelihood that the message will be retained has just increased from 10 percent to approximately 50 percent.

Organization

Visual aids help you to organize your material. They help keep you on track and ensure that all the information is covered. We must keep in mind, however, that the visual aids do not drive the speech or presentation. You have already written the speech or prepared the outline, and the visual aids are placed strategically within that framework to enhance the presentation. As an organizational tool, visuals are also a way for you to guide the audience. When you use each visual to present a key point, for example, the audience is better able to follow the organization of the speech. As a result, you are more persuasive, look better prepared, and appear to be more competent.

Understanding

The use of visual aids promotes understanding. They enable you to illustrate the spoken idea with graphs, charts, pictures, or key words. This is particularly valuable if you are explaining concepts or somewhat complex information. For example, you might be making a presentation involving a lot of figures and statistics. The information will be more interesting and meaningful if you present it in charts and graphs rather than in rows and columns of numbers.

Support

Visual aids support your words and message by stimulating the audience's senses. Today's easy access to computer-generated graphics enables presenters to enhance their messages with interesting colors, pictures, motion, and sound.

Emphasis

Although you may use the various verbal techniques to emphasize key points, many people in the audience may still not be attuned to your use of emphasis. For example, the speaker may say something like, "The first important point is . . . " or, "I can't stress enough the importance of . . . " or, "Now that we've addressed the causes, let's look at the effects." Given that most people are not good listeners and that many people process information through different modalities, the key point on a visual helps place the emphasis where the speaker intends it to be. Consequently, there should be no doubt about the importance of that piece of information.

GUIDELINES FOR USING VISUAL AIDS

Regardless of which visual aid you use, the following guidelines will help you to create visuals that get the results you want.

Limit Their Use

First, don't use too many visuals. I have seen presentations that are nothing but one screen, slide, or transparency after another. Keep in mind the point made earlier that the visual is an aid, not your entire presentation.

Keep It Simple

Nothing is more annoying than looking at a transparency, for example, that has been made directly from a page of 12-point text and crammed with lines and lines of information. Make sure you observe the principle of putting only one idea on each visual and no more than one illustration. There should be only six or seven words per line and six or seven lines per visual. Some speakers who have recently discovered the myriad of options available through computer software programs tend to go overboard by doing too much. Remember that less is much more effective.

Make It Easy to Read

Each visual should be seen clearly by the entire audience. Use type no smaller than 18-point or three inches high when projected.

Use Color

Color is more effective than black-and-white for a variety of reasons. First, it has more cognitive impact. People simply remember color. As a result, your visual is more interesting, has more impact, and makes a greater impression. In a study conducted by the Bureau of Advertising, results showed that ads in color increased retention from 55 percent to 78 percent. With the availability of color printers and other pieces of technology, using color is easy. Another important consideration is that audiences expect color. Even classic black-and-white films have been "colorized." Why? Because audiences are turned off by black-and-white. However, please keep in mind that many people are color-blind. It has been estimated that 20 percent of men cannot distinguish some colors, causing colored objects or words to appear as shades of gray, black, and white, varying only in degrees of lightness and darkness.

Use It and Lose It

Because the visual is an aid, it should be visible only when it is relevant to the point being made. In other words, when you are finished with the aid, remove it or turn it off. Otherwise, the audience will continue to focus on the visual and will pay little or no attention to what you are saying. People are easily distracted as it is, so don't give them anything else to divert them from your important message.

COMMONLY USED VISUAL AIDS

Flip Chart Pad and Easel

When discussing the use of the flip chart, we need to address two different applications: (1) prepared pages and (2) blank pages on which the speaker or trainer captures information spontaneously throughout the session. Let's start with prepared pages.

Prepared pages are used the same way as slides or transparencies, but they tend to communicate a more casual approach or create a more casual atmosphere. A major advantage of prepared pages is that you can take the time to make sure the printing is neat and legible. This is particularly important if you have a problem writing legibly. Another advantage is that valuable session time is not spent at the easel—you are able to show the information quickly and move on. As with other forms of visual aids, the pages double as notes for the presenter.

For blank pages used to present or capture information as you move through the session, there are also some important dos and don'ts. First, if you have asked for input from audience members and are capturing their responses, it is imperative that you write down exactly what each audience member has said. Do not capture the information in your own words. What if the person responding has a difficult time making his or her point succinctly? Some people do go on and on. There are two different approaches you can use. After listening intently to the person's response, ask the individual to summarize his or her point in a few words so you can capture it on the page. If, however, the person isn't able to condense his or her point, ask if you might paraphrase what you heard and ask permission to write it down. As Bob Pike says, "People don't argue with their own data," but they may argue with yours, so make sure you are respectful of their words and intent.

In full-day or half-day sessions, it is a good idea to tear off the pages and tape them to the wall. Before doing so, however, put a brief descriptive title at the top of each sheet. To save time, cut one-inch masking tape into several two- to three-inch lengths before the session begins. That will enable you to post the pages quickly. Depending on the wall covering, you might also be able to use push pins. Some hotels and conference centers will not allow you to put anything on the walls, so be sure to check with the meeting planner or facilities coordinator for permission. Otherwise, you might end up with a bill for repainting or new wallpaper. If you are not permitted to use tape or pins, a safe alternative is to use a magnetic dry-erase easel pad that clings to most wall surfaces. You can easily position and reposition individual sheets on the wall using no tape or tacks. The pages are erasable and reusable with dry-erase markers and won't bleed through. I always carry a rolled up pad in my car just in case the meeting planner forgot to order a flip chart or if I'm in a room with a troublesome wall surface. Whatever you do, don't write on the page after it is posted on the wall—many markers have a tendency to bleed through! If you are using the blank page to write down points as you go, you may want to prepare some pages ahead of time in light pencil so you will not have to look at your notes. This is especially helpful if you have complex material. Just think how brilliant your audience will think you are—you don't have to refer to your notes.

GENERAL GUIDELINES FOR WRITING ON THE PAD

Whichever method of flip-chart use you choose, the following guidelines will help you project a polished, professional image to your audience:

- Limit your use of the flip chart to relatively small groups of no more than 25 or 30.
- Print in block letters three to four inches high so that everyone in the room can see your information.
- Don't put more than about 10 lines of information on a page.
- Don't fill the page to the bottom. Since people are sitting, their vertical range of vision is somewhat limited.
- Don't talk to the easel while you are writing.
- Wait at least 20 to 30 seconds after you finish writing before you flip the page so that people can take down the information if they wish.
- Don't stand in front of the easel after you have finished writing. Once again, give people an opportunity to capture the information.
- Consider using two or more easels across the front of the room when you must develop a continuous, uninterrupted flow of ideas or can't post pages on the wall.
- If possible, choose easel pads of white paper with perforated sheet tops for easy tearing. Don't use flip-chart paper with lines on it—it looks unprofessional.

- Use a wide, felt-tip, watercolor marker that will not bleed through the paper.
- Be mindful of the impact of color and use blue, green, brown, and black to add variety and interest. Save red for emphasis.
- Alternate colors by lines to make reading easier.
- Use colors systematically: one for page heading, one for primary points, another for subpoints.
- When you are not writing, put the pen down.

OVERHEAD PROJECTOR AND TRANSPARENCIES

Transparencies are great for medium-sized audiences. They are easy to make and to use. Just like any other visual aid, they can be misused and abused quite easily.

Preparing Transparencies

There are several ways to create transparencies—a method for every pocketbook.

1. At the very low end, you can buy a box of clear transparencies and write in colored markers right on the acetate.
2. You can purchase a box of colored transparencies made especially for either a laser printer or a photo copier. If using a laser printer, your text, of course, is generated from your computer and instead of printing it on paper, you load your transparency. You might also have a piece of printed material from which you would like to make a transparency. In that case, once again, substitute the transparency film for your paper in your copier. In both cases, the background will be colored, but the print will be black.
3. Some people prefer colored lettering. If that's the case, several options are available. One option is to purchase a color printer for your computer and generate the docu-

ment. Another option is to purchase a thermal copier and different boxes of heat sensitive thermal film of various types. For example, a rainbow assortment is available, allowing you to create red, blue, green, or purple print on a clear background. You can also buy blue film that produces yellow print on a blue background and black film that gives you a black background and clear lettering. You can then create different colored lettering on the black background by putting different colored pieces of acetate behind the clear lettering.

4. Another interesting "create-as-you-go" option is to buy special ColorBurst™ Write-On film and ColorBurst™ markers that produce a colored image on a royal blue background. This option works much like the flip-chart pages that you use to capture or present information as you go. This method has the advantage of being somewhat unique and it therefore captures the audience's attention more than does the flip chart that most people are used to.

5. At the upper end of the cost continuum are the professionally prepared transparencies. There are many mail-order service bureaus offering custom transparency and slide generation and an increasing number of walk-in service shops, such as Kinko's. Depending on your purpose and the number of times you intend to use the transparencies, you may choose to go this route. You can generate your own text on your computer and send the disk to the servicer, or you can ask the servicer to create the transparencies or slides for you.

Guidelines for Better Transparencies

The transparency presents some unique advantages as well as important challenges. Here are some guidelines for getting the most out of this visual aid.

Creativity
The nature of the transparency lends itself to creativity. In addition to the different types of film mentioned earlier, you

can create your own "active" transparency resulting from a layering effect. For example, you could create a transparency with your key words and then cut the film apart so you have several "minitransparencies." Then you would create a hinge effect by laying each word on the projector as you announce or refer to it.

Framing

Professionals who use transparencies make sure each one is framed. Framing a transparency blocks unnecessary light, provides rigidity, makes the film easier to handle, and creates a more polished appearance. Once again, you have options, depending on cost and personal preference. One way to go is to purchase a box of cardboard frames on which you mount the transparency with transparent tape. Another option would be to purchase an Instaframe, which is a plastic frame with a glass insert. All you do is place the frame on the platform of the overhead projector and place the individual transparencies on and take them off as you use them. This enables you to keep your transparencies any way you choose and you don't have to continue to purchase frames. A third framing option is the 3M Company FlipFrame™. The FlipFrame™ is a transparent sleeve in which you insert the transparency. It has hinged flaps that, when flipped out, form a frame around the transparency and provide room for notes no one else can see. FlipFrames™ are hole-punched along the left side so you can put them in a binder for better organization and protection.

Control

I'm sure we have all been in presentations at which the overhead projector became an annoyance because the presenter did not control its use properly. For example, the audience should never have to look at a blank screen with a blinding light. Put the transparency on the platform, then turn on the

projector. Turn the projector off before you remove the transparency. Some people argue that if you have a number of
transparencies, the process of turning the screen on and off
becomes a nuisance to both the presenter and the audience.
Once again, there are ways around this annoyance and inconvenience. You could cut a square of heavy paper or cardboard
the size of the lens aperture and attach it with masking tape
in hinge-like fashion to the top of the lens casing. Then,
rather than turning the projector off between transparencies,
you simply bring down the hinged cover, thus creating a black
screen. Similarly, you can lay a sheet of paper or cardboard on
the platform to block the light. You can also purchase a
remote device from an electronics store that enables you to
turn the projector on and off from several feet away. This is
particularly effective if you are going to talk at some length
before showing the next transparency or if you have moved
into the audience and don't want to break the mood by
returning to the front of the room to turn off the projector.

Another aspect of control involves the way in which you
use the overhead projector. The purpose of the overhead projector is to allow the presenter to show the visual while interacting with the audience. You can call attention to specific
points on the transparency without ever turning your back
on the audience. There are several ways you can direct the
audience's attention using the transparency. One way is to
cover the transparency with a sheet of paper and as you make
your point, uncover each word or line on the transparency.
That way, your audience will read only what you want them
to read and when. You may want to use a pointer or pen to
point to key words on the transparency. Any standard or
retractable pointer will do but you might want to make
things more interesting by purchasing hand pointers like the
one used and sold by Bob Pike. Pike's version is a miniature
plastic hand attached to a narrow wooden stick. Chris Clarke
Epstein also uses and sells a hand pointer. Her version is a

narrow piece of plexiglass with one end cut in the shape of a hand with a pointing finger and the other end shaped like an arrow. I have listed major suppliers of training tools in the resource section at the end of the book.

Still another method of calling attention to specific information on the transparency is to use a transparency marker to underline or circle key points as you go. One word of advice: Absolutely never point at the screen! I was in a meeting once in which a bank CEO was presenting the financial report to all the bank officers. The fact that he had no clue as to the proper use of the overhead projector was magnified when he pointed to the screen with his silver retractable pointer and put a hole right in the middle of the screen! The last small piece of advice concerning the overhead projector is to dim the lights near the screen to create a sharp contrast and to make it easier for the audience to see the visual.

USING VIDEO AND VIDEO CLIPS

Speakers use videos and video clips depending on a variety of factors, including length of session, type of audience, and cost of the video. Let's look first at the use of videos in a seminar or training session.

A common mistake made by speakers and trainers when using videos is that they give a brief introduction to the video, show it, and then conduct a brief discussion afterward. The problem is that too often only a small number of people participate in the discussion, and some audience members think this is a perfect opportunity to catch up on a little sleep. The use of videos can be made more meaningful with a little forethought and preparation. First, be clear about your reason for using the video. What purpose is the video to serve? Is it the best way to communicate your point, or are you using it to take up time? Preview the video at least twice and make sure it is up-to-date and does not contain anything offensive. For example, does it reflect diversity? Take notes and develop handouts or other learning aids. When introducing the video, be sure to provide adequate background and explain anything that may be a bit unusual. Many people may not be familiar with certain accents or types of humor. Prepare them appropriately by letting them know what to look for and maybe even by giving specific assignments to specific parts of the audience. After showing the video, discuss the video's main points and how they relate to your topic. There are creative ways of getting full participation from the audience, and we will discuss these methods in subsequent chapters. Provide a summary and conclusion and then bridge to the next part of your presentation.

Video clips, on the other hand, are used more in shorter sessions, even keynotes. Many of the same guidelines apply here as well. Once again, you have several options. You might want to use a small portion from a movie or television show to illustrate your point. This is a great idea and very effective, but be sure to get written permission. Copyright laws are not to be taken lightly. There are, however, libraries of copyright-free video clips you can use in your presentation. And don't forget news clips and other events captured on film that are in the public domain. A way around the cost and inconvenience of dealing with copyrighted material is to create your own video clips. They can be as professional or as amateurish as you want. Here is an opportunity for aspiring or nonprofessional actors to get both experience and exposure. You might write your own script and use your friends, clients, or acting students from the local college or university to illustrate your points, skills, or concepts through short vignettes.

COMPUTER-BASED MEDIA

Computer-generated slides take the place of transparencies and 35mm slides. The equipment requirements include a computer, an LCD panel with an overhead projector, or an LCD projector. Computer capabilities enable you to create professional and polished shows with animation, sound, special effects, and even video enhancements. The flexibility of the media enables you to modify information on a moment's notice to reflect late-breaking developments or audience input. On the down side, equipment is expensive, and because the technology is changing so rapidly, equipment becomes outdated fairly quickly. Another problem is that the hotel or convention center may not have the necessary equipment available, which means you must lug heavy and cumbersome equipment with you. Consequently, there is increased potential for equipment to become lost or damaged. You will find more detailed information about computer-based media in one of the other books in *The Essence of Public Speaking Series, TechEdge: Using Computers Present and Persuade,* by William J. Ringle.

HANDOUTS

Yes, believe it or not, handouts are visual aids, and their use must be as carefully considered and orchestrated as that of any other visual. No matter how short your presentation or speech, I strongly believe that you should have at least a one-page handout with key points or an outline. For one thing, many people like to take notes. For another, a handout helps guide the audience. Finally, a handout is much more likely to help audience members remember you.

How to use handouts, when to use them, and how much information should be included is up to you. It depends on the length of your session, its purpose, and what you want a handout to accomplish.

Some speakers believe that if they give the audience a handout, people will spend time reading the handout and not listening to what the speaker has to say. If that's your philosophy, then you may not want to distribute your hand-out until after the session. If you choose that approach, be sure to tell the audience members at the beginning of your presentation that they don't have to take notes because you will be providing a handout containing key points at the end of the program.

For other speakers, particularly those who conduct half-day or full-day sessions, handouts are a must and are distributed at the beginning of the session. They are used as a workbook to guide and direct the participants. Once again, individual philosophy dictates how extensive the handout is. Some speakers provide thick manuals containing lots of information; others provide little detail but lots of space for participants to write down thoughts, ideas, or responses to discussion questions or activities. Regardless of which approach you choose, your handout should look professional. That means the typeface and fonts are consistent. Choose large, simple typefaces, and use bold headings to attract attention and to make a point. Also, be sure to double space between paragraphs and use bullets for lists. With the ease and availability of desktop publishing, there should be no excuse for a speaker throwing together a number of pieces that have clearly come from different sources. If possible, include graphics and other illustrations to make the pages more interesting.

SPECIAL CHALLENGES

When preparing all visuals, particularly handouts, be sensitive to people in the audience who may be visually impaired. I was asked to do a session for residents and staff from a number of retirement communities. In talking with the meeting planner, I learned that the audience would be roughly a 50–50 mix between residents and staff. I also learned that 80 was the average age of the residents. With that in mind, I prepared the handouts in larger type and left more space between sections.

THE SPEAKER AS A VISUAL AID

Believe it or not, the speaker can also be considered a visual aid. Although what you say (verbal) and how you say it (vocal) are the essence of who you are as a speaker, you cannot overlook the power of your physical presence (visual) and its impact on the audience. You can use your physical presence to enhance your message and increase your effectiveness.

Physical Appearance

People form an impression of you within the first few seconds—as soon as you walk on stage or enter the room. That impression is lasting and often determines how members of the audience react to you. I learned a powerful lesson about physical appearance early in my speaking and training career. I was speaking to a group of about 35 bank branch managers in an all-day seminar. The audience responded well to me, and I thought everyone was pleased with the session. My assumptions were confirmed as I quickly scanned the evaluations until I came upon an evaluation from a man who gave me very poor marks essentially because he didn't like my red suit. Not only did he go on and on about the inappropriate wearing of the color red, but also he went to the meeting planner and complained to her. She defended my choice of clothing by pointing out that she had suggested I wear something bright because I was presenting in a large, tiered lecture hall with a black background and the audience would have a difficult time seeing me. The man remained adamant. He said he had attended a seminar in which he learned that red is an aggressive color, and therefore, he felt a speaker should not be displaying such aggressive tendencies to her audience. In a similar situation—same location, different audience—another man gave me a scathing review because he did not like my eye makeup and was distracted by it during the entire session. The lesson here is that although we have no way to predict how our physical appearance will affect individual people in our audiences, we can take measures to minimize any negative impact.

Guidelines for Dress and Make-up

Three words should guide you in your selection of dress for your speaking engagements: *professional, appropriate, comfortable*. First and foremost, keep in mind that you are a professional, and that's the image you want to project at all times. Men should stick to navy, gray, and black suits with white or colored shirts and a good silk tie. Women have more choices. Depending on the situation, women may choose a dark suit and then accent it with a brightly colored blouse. It is also appropriate for a woman to wear a bright business suit in royal blue, emerald green, or sapphire, for example. Be sure that the colors you choose are appropriate for your color wheel and style as well as the occasion and room conditions. For example, I look better in "winter" colors, such as royal, emerald, sapphire, fuschia, and red as well as navy or black. I fade out in pastels or earth tones. If you are appearing on a stage with stage lighting in front of a large audience, your choice of dress and makeup will need to be more dramatic.

A good rule of thumb is to dress equal to or above the level of your audience. If, for example, your audience is dressed in business casual, then you, too, should dress accordingly but go one step beyond a skirt or slacks and a sweater. Add a blazer or sport coat. Above all, make sure your clothing is comfortable and fits well. Avoid wearing anything distracting. This is a particular concern for woman and their accessories. Do not wear bangle bracelets or dangling earrings; both become a distraction rather than an enhancement. Once again, however, if you are addressing a large audience, you may choose to wear larger button earrings that sparkle or catch the light. Gold and silver are both great, and depending on the setting, you may also want to use something glittery. Shoes are another consideration. Men's choices are pretty limited—slip-ons or tied. That choice is determined by the degree of casualness of the rest of your attire. Women, however, can choose flats or heels of varying height. This becomes a matter of personal preference and comfort, particularly if you are going to be conducting an all-day seminar or workshop. Do not wear very high heels. They change your center of gravity, cause you to walk and stand differently, and do not provide you with the stability and balance you need in front of an audience.

Because you want the audience to look at your face while you are speaking, speech coach Mary Beth Roach recommends that speakers use white powder around their eyes to draw people's attention up.

Above all else, you want people to concentrate on what you are saying, not on what you're wearing. (Remember my red suit story?) If you keep in mind the words *professional, appropriate,* and *comfortable,* you'll never go wrong.

BODY LANGUAGE, GESTURES, MOVEMENT, AND FACIAL EXPRESSION

Your body language, gestures, movement, and facial expression all contribute to the impression your listeners form of you. They can either encourage them to or discourage them from hearing your message.

Posture

Let's start with posture. Always stand straight with feet shoulder width apart to give you balance. If you stand with your feet close together, you will have a tendency to sway. Whatever you do, don't lean on the lectern. I observed in horror as a speaker made the mistake of leaning on a portable, desk-top lectern which promptly sailed off the table and crashed to the floor. If you are not gesturing, keep your hands to your side.

Gestures

Gestures are very effective means of emphasizing your points. Gestures should be natural, meaningful, and controlled. In other words, don't fling your arms wildly or use your hands and arms in a robotic manner. Particularly in front of a large audience, use bigger gestures than you normally would, and with today's diverse audiences, make sure none of your gestures are offensive. When you extend your arm and hand in a pointing gesture, be sure to keep your fingers together. In other words, use your entire hand rather than one finger to point. Also remember that sharp, sudden gestures create negative emotions.

Movement

Make your movement meaningful. Your movement should be one fluid motion: step, cross, plant. Although movement is a matter of style, be aware of the impact it can have on your audience. At one extreme, we have the statue, the speaker who stays in one place and never moves. Although certainly not distracting, this "visual aid" is uninteresting. At the other extreme is the speaker who is in constant motion, who never stays in one place for more than a minute. Not only is this behavior distracting to audience members, they will probably feel worn out or exhausted by the end of your presentation. I was hired recently to speak at a board retreat for a chapter of Meeting Professionals International (MPI). The meeting planner who engaged me had also hired me five years ago for a presentation to a chapter of ASAE (American Society of Association Executives). After the MPI presentation, she was extremely complimentary, telling me that I was right on target in meeting their needs. Then she commented that my style is so much different from what it was five years ago. She said that what she remembered from my ASAE presentation was not what I said but what I did. She told me that I was constantly moving, and she had found that not only distracting but also indicating a lack of confidence. She went on to say that this time I exuded self-confidence, limited my movement, engaged in more eye contact, and interacted with the audience. What great feedback! Try to find a happy medium. Decide where you want to move to and go there. Plant your feet and continue talking. We will address where you should move to and why when we take a look at theatrical techniques in Chapter 5.

Facial Expression

As a personal visual aid, we cannot overlook the importance of your facial expression. From the first moment the audience sees you, they should feel warmth emanating from the platform. The easiest and most effective way of achieving this is to smile—smile with both your mouth and your eyes. A smile communicates to your audience, "I'm really glad to be here. I like you and I hope you'll like me." Throughout your speech or presentation, your facial expressions can help or hinder your message. Make sure they are congruent with your words. You certainly would not want to frown if you were saying something meant to be positive and upbeat. What people see is more powerful than what they hear.

An important consideration for the interactive speaker is that the lower the technology, the more interactive you can be. So choose your media carefully.

Speaking as a Performing Art

According to professional speaker Scott McKain, "The speaking business is show business." That means we, as speakers, must learn to do things a little differently; that is, we can no longer expect to satisfy an audience just by speaking. One of our goals should be to project confidence and warmth along with sincerity. We must recognize and adapt to the fact that speaking is indeed a performing art. We are on stage each time we speak, regardless of the venue. Furthermore, we have only a minute or two to grab an audience's attention, establish rapport, and make audience members feel it is worth their time and money to be there.

With that in mind, let's look at some specific staging techniques to help you interact more effectively with your audience.

THE STAGE OR PLATFORM

Let's start with the stage. In many cases, this is personal preference; in others, it's a matter of necessity depending on the room, the size of the audience, the type of presentation, and the speaker's height. Many professionals suggest using a platform or riser, if possible. This is particularly important for those of us who are short. Experts recommend a 14-inch riser for a small audience and a 24-inch riser for audiences of over 100 people. Others prefer to be *with* the audience, literally on its level. They believe that a stage or elevated area creates a distance between the speaker and the audience. Real pros can overcome that barrier and bridge the gap by using many of the interactive techniques we will address in Chapters 6, 7, and 8.

POSITION AND MOVEMENT

Every stage or platform area can be seen as laid out in sections or a grid (see Figure 5.1). The mood you want to convey and the strength of your message should determine your placement or position on that stage. The strongest position is downstage center. This position should be used to deliver your most important point. Downstage right is where you want to tell a touching story or create an intimate feeling with the audience. Upstage center is also a strong position but, because it places the speaker farther from the audience, it also creates an emotional distance. If you want to deliver a light or humorous story, you should move to downstage left. Both

Figure 5.1

Sections of the Platform

Speaker		
Upstage right	Upstage center	Upstage left
Downstage right	Downstage center	Downstage left
Audience		

upstage right and upstage left are undesirable spots, and it is advisable for speakers to refrain from going to those spots.

Many professional speakers believe that every movement should be carefully planned and thought out and that you should "block" your speech just as you would a play. Movement should be purposeful. Plan where you want to go, go there, plant your feet firmly, and deliver your message. Take long strides and make the stage your own by taking up lots of space through movement and gestures.

LIGHTING

Lighting is a very effective way of creating a mood and of focusing the audience's attention. Spotlights are very powerful, focusing full attention on the speaker. There are drawbacks, however. If you tend to move around a lot, the lighting technician may have a difficult time following you, and you could easily find yourself "in the dark." On the other hand, if the spotlight's range of motion is limited, you, too, will be limited in your movement. Rather than spotlights, some speakers prefer a softer look created through the use of blue and pink gel lights.

THE SOUND OF MUSIC

Music and sound are nice touches. Many speakers use music to set a tone, create a mood, or evoke an emotion that spoken words alone cannot convey. There are a number of speakers who are also talented musicians, singers, or dancers, and they incorporate their musical talent very effectively into their presentations. If you are blessed with these other talents, use them, but make sure you are using the art to enhance your speech or presentation. In other words, the music should not be your main purpose or focus. As an important word of caution, be certain you are talented. I have witnessed some speakers who failed miserably because they had limited talent in these areas. As a result, the message was lost because the only thing the audience remembered was the speaker's embarrassingly feeble attempt to sing, dance, or play an instrument.

If you are not talented in these areas, don't despair. There are other ways of incorporating music into your presentation. You might want to use taped music recorded by a professional. Many speakers have music played while they are approaching the stage or platform and as they leave. This music might come to be associated with a particular speaker, much like a signature story. If you would like to sing but can't carry a tune, you could also lip sync to a well-known song.

When playing prerecorded music, be very careful not to violate copyright laws. You will have to pay royalties for the use of music protected by copyright. In most cases, it is the client organization's responsibility to pay the appropriate licensing fee. If you don't want to deal with paying to use music, you have other options. You might commission someone to compose a song or piece of music for you on a work-for-hire basis. You, then, would own the rights to use the piece whenever and wherever you wanted. You could also peruse music libraries and select music in the public domain. A song is often the best way to create the emotional impact you want, so don't shy away from using it just because of licensing restrictions. Contact professional societies such as ASCAP (American Society of Composers, Authors, and Publishers) and/or BMI (Broadcast Music Incorporated) to learn more about licensing agreements.

Be sure to cue your piece of music so it starts exactly when and where you want it to. An even better way to avoid confusion and prevent any mix-up is to record one piece per tape and clearly label each one.

STEP PLACEMENT

The placement of the steps leading to the platform will depend on how you plan to interact with the audience. Steps at the side will give you a graceful and unobtrusive way to enter and exit the platform. It's also a useful location for bringing audience members onto the stage. Placement of the steps at the front of the stage is important if you plan to step off the stage and move into the audience.

MICROPHONES

Microphones are another important consideration. The selection of a microphone is a matter of personal choice—depending on your style and the type of presentation you are giving. The real pros often use their own microphones.

To avoid the distraction of dodging cords or, even worse, tripping over them, request a cordless handheld or lavaliere microphone. For optimum freedom of movement, particularly if you use a lot of props, choose a lavaliere. Cordless models require a transmitter box that you put in your pocket or hook on your waist in the back so it does not mar your appearance with an unsightly bulge. Be sure to take this into consideration when planning what to wear. Women, for example, should plan to wear a suit rather than a dress so you have some place to hook the transmitter and conceal it from your audience.

If you get stuck using a lavaliere microphone with a cord, take necessary steps to avoid potential problems with the cord. For example, run the cord up and underneath your suit jacket. Otherwise, you run the risk of catching the cord with your hands or sleeve and detaching the microphone clip. I observed a new speaker during a conference breakout session do just that. She had the cord on the outside of her jacket, and every time she brought her arm up to gesture, she pulled the microphone clip off her lapel. During the hour-long session, this happened a number of times, distracting the audience and embarrassing the speaker.

USING PROPS TO PROP UP YOUR AUDIENCE

The use of props is becoming increasingly popular. Prop master and NSA member Tim Gard defines a prop as "anything that enhances, strengthens, or reinforces an audience's ability to visualize, accept, or understand a concept." Although props are visual aids and are used for a purpose similar to those aids mentioned in Chapter 4, I am including them in this chapter because of their unique relationship to the theater and show business. According to Gard, props fall into the following categories:

- **Enhancers.** These are lower-level props used solely to enhance mental images. They can be visual, sound-only, or both.
- **Theatrical.** These props assist the audience in realizing the image. They include items such as wigs, hats, costumes, and magic tricks.
- **Giveaways.** These are items, full-size or miniature versions, that you give to people in the audience. Their purpose is to heighten awareness and promote you and your program or product.
- **Signature.** These items can be either props or giveaways associated with a particular speaker.

Before I go into detail, I must emphasize that the prop examples that the speakers who use them were kind enough to share are considered signature props. In fact, some speakers have copyrighted their usage of a particular item. My purpose in including these ideas is to illustrate the concept of selecting a prop or giveaway and using it to illustrate a point you are making and to leave an indelible impression with your audience. So, please, do not borrow these signature ideas or gimmicks.

Props are an easy and economical theatrical technique that will get the audience's attention and help you communicate your message. Props appeal especially to the visual modality. They help reinforce the speaker's message by relating the visual image to the spoken word. The image will last long after the words are forgotten. For example, when I speak to audiences about professional image, I begin by holding up two boxes of the same shape and size. One box is professionally wrapped with attractive paper and coordinating ribbon and bow; the other is wrapped in haphazard fashion in aluminum foil and tied with white curling ribbon. I ask the audience to indicate with a show of hands which package they would like to receive. Almost everyone chooses the attractive package. (Of course, there are always a few who choose the other—just to make things interesting.) I then ask one or two people to tell me (and the rest of the audience) why they prefer the professionally wrapped box to the other. They mention, of course, that it is more aesthetically appealing. This provides the segue into my points about professional image:

- Image is a matter of perception.
- Successful people first decide how they want to be perceived.
- Then they determine what they need to do to create that perception.

It's amazing how much of an impact that simple prop has on the audience. I have had people who had been in the audience approach me months and even years after that particular presentation and tell me that they still remember "the boxes" and the impression that image made on them.

In her speech "Life Is a Presentation: There Are No Dress Rehearsals," Marjorie Brody uses a hotel towel as a visual metaphor for perception. Like many speakers, Brody spends many nights in hotels. She brings two towels on stage and talks about how her perception of the hotel is determined by the towels in the bathroom. Holding up a large, plush towel, she explains that if the towel is large, fluffy, white, smells fresh, and feels soft against her skin, she has a favorable impression of the hotel. She then picks up a small, flimsy towel and tells the audience that if the towel is small and feels coarse to the touch, she braces herself for a less-than-enjoyable stay. Brody makes the point that we are similar to the towels, and the perception others may have of us may be based on initial impressions.

Props and Points

Coming up with prop ideas is not difficult. The key is to sit down and think about your major theme and brainstorm what objects might relate to or represent that particular theme or message. When I speak about coaching to improve workplace performance, I take with me to the platform a teddy bear dressed as an athletic coach. He is attired in a baseball cap and polo shirt and has a whistle around his neck. The teddy bear has added significance for me personally because I collect teddy bears. I use my "coach" bear to introduce the concept of coaching and how coaches in the work environment are similar to coaches in the world of sports.

During management development programs or presentations, I speak about employee motivation. To make my point about the different approaches to motivating employees, I bring in three props: a whip, a carrot dangling at the end of a stick, and a flowering plant. I show the whip to illustrate threats managers often make to try to get employees to perform better. The carrot on the stick represents incentive programs or promises of rewards as a motivational tool. The flowering plant is a metaphor for an environment in which people are motivated. To get a plant to bloom, you must use the right amount of water, light, temperature, and fertilizer, and each plant requires different care. The same is true for people. Successful managers will understand the different "care" required by each of their employees and will create an appropriate environment accordingly. My "motivation" props are always a big hit. The audience laughs, and in training programs, participants frequently refer to the props throughout the session.

One word of caution: make sure your props can be seen. The larger the audience, the larger the prop. When I speak about organizational change and the importance of launching a comprehensive organization development initiative, I sometimes bring out a 36-inch bandage to emphasize that organizations often use a "Band-Aid™" approach to solving problems instead of initiating a top-down, full-scale, and well-planned change effort. I also use a giant Slinky™ magic spring to illustrate the importance of remaining flexible and adapting to change and a kaleidoscope to represent the changing environment. To encourage people to look at things differently, I give out Magic Eye™ postcards. I use puzzle pieces for team building, giving each team member a puzzle piece, which he or she holds until the end of the session, when I ask all of the team members to get up and put their pieces together to complete the puzzle. I remind them that they are individuals but that they also must all come together to form the whole.

For my program on "The Art of Influencing," I use a huge artist's palette to illustrate that mastering interpersonal skills is indeed an art. Just as the painter chooses the right mix of colors from the palette, we, as human beings interacting with others, must choose the right mix of strategies to enhance our interpersonal effectiveness.

I often use a magic wand, "magic dust" (that is, glitter), or a crystal ball. In a management development session, I might mention that people are promoted to management positions and someone sprinkles "magic dust" or waves a magic wand, and "abracadabra!" they now know how to manage. The crystal ball can be used in a career development program to make a point that many people expect to look into a crystal ball and see their futures rather than take control of their careers by developing a plan and managing it.

When you have audience members participate in role plays in front of the group (more about that later), you can use a film director's clapboard to stop the action to coach the participant or to have other participants give feedback.

Posters of quotations related to the topic can be displayed around the meeting room to create a mood and to generate interest in the topic. I often use these quotations at the beginning of a session by asking participants to choose a quotation from those posted and explain how it relates to them. For example, in a time management session, I display the following quotations:

■ Money lost can be replaced but time lost is gone forever.
■ People who have half an hour to spend usually spend it with someone who hasn't.
■ Everybody has the problem of time; for of all resources, it is the scarcest, the most perishable, and the most elusive.

NSA member Don Blohowiak makes an impact on audiences when he talks about the information-gathering process by showing up with his "tool belt" portable office, from which he pulls out a cellular telephone, electronic note taker, index cards, recorder, scissors, four-color pen, and highlighter. Blohowiak also uses a magic wand when he speaks on empowerment. Getting his audience to think about and define the term, he walks around waving the magic wand over various participants' heads, telling them that they are now "empowered." The audience gets a good laugh, and it makes a powerful point that empowerment doesn't happen like magic; it takes a lot of work and commitment on the part of managers. In his sessions on change management, he uses a red pom-pom to illustrate that organizations going through change sometimes resort to the "rah-rah" cheerleading approach in introducing change to their employees. Blohowiak also uses an eight-foot bullwhip, which he cracks loudly to illustrate the type of controlling organizational authority by which many people have managed through the years. According to Blohowiak, "Props reduce an important point to the comic level, making it easier for the audience to relate. It also makes the point tangible and makes an impression more powerful than words alone can do."

GIVEAWAYS

The prop carried onto the stage or platform becomes even more effective and memorable if you have "giveaways" and/or handouts that coordinate with your theme. For example, I might give my audience members whistles like the one worn by "coach" bear or bandages like the one I use to remind people not to use a "Band-Aid™" approach to solving organizational ills. My signature giveaways for the "Art of Influencing" include silver artist palette pins and chocolate candy in the shape of a palette. I give miniature Slinkies™ to remind people to be flexible and kaleidoscopes to help them look at things differently. My handouts will include that particular image on the cover page and throughout the handout packet.

Former NSA president Mike McKinley uses a mirror to encourage the members in his audiences to "look inside themselves." McKinley also uses bottles of Wite-Out® correction fluid to help people "correct their mistakes." Mikki Williams uses a purple rubber band with red lettering (her signature colors) in her sessions on goal setting. In some of her sessions, she gives each audience member a ruler and asks them to break the ruler in half and take the pieces home with them as a reminder that we need to "break the rules" from time to time.

Several speakers I know speak on stress management. Some speakers give participants stress balloons and others give "Stress Meter" cards. You can order both the balloons and the cards through a number of promotional products catalogues. I have included several sources of these and other promotional products in the resource section of the book. I use stress dots, which I place on each participant's hand at the beginning of the session. Both the cards and the dots change color as a person's body temperature changes. Throughout the session, participants can monitor their own stress levels by observing how the dots (or cards) change color. Toward the end of my session, I take participants through a deep relaxation exercise and show them how they can use the stress dots as a biofeedback tool.

Cube puzzles can be used to represent problem solving, and jigsaw puzzles are great for communicating interdependence of team members in a team-building session. In sessions on goal setting, I give out mini compasses to represent staying on course.

Props don't always have to be representative objects. Sometimes just holding up items such as books, newspaper clippings, or magazine articles can be very effective. The audience doesn't need to see what's actually written. All it needs to see is that the article is authentic. This type of prop becomes even more effective if the speaker quotes a few words from it. Because your article or clipping will get a lot of use, be sure to laminate it so it will not become worn or be destroyed.

If you choose to use props, have a small table set to the side of the platform within easy reach. Arrange them in order of use so you won't forget which item to use when and you won't fumble trying to find it.

USING THEMES

The client may have a theme or you may choose to create one yourself as a metaphor for your topic. You would then decorate the room and choose props and giveaways to support the theme. For example, I often use the metaphor of a sailboat cruise to represent team building. The meeting room is decorated in a nautical theme and when participants arrive, volunteers place leis around participants' necks and give out compasses to help them "stay on course." Each person also receives a sea creature eraser and a roll of LifeSavers™ candies.

You might have a space theme and have the room darkened and decorated with glow-in-the-dark stars and other celestial objects. If you were doing a session dealing with group problem solving or decision making, you would choose one of the outer-space survival simulations as a group exercise, dealing with group decision making and problem solving as well as other space-related activities.

CHARACTERS AND COSTUMES

We have already addressed the role of the speaker's attire in creating an impact on the audience. In this chapter, however, we will look specifically at the use of costumes. Several professional speakers communicate their messages through the character and persona of a well-known personality or historical figure. For example, Ralph Archbold speaks on change and creativity through the persona of Ben Franklin. Archbold dresses in period costume like Franklin, speaks with an accent, and totally assumes the character of one of America's most beloved forefathers. He is so believable in his appearance and demeanor that audience members are immediately engaged and almost believe they are watching and listening to Ben Franklin in person.

Mary Beth Roach, a motivational speaker, does a Mae West impersonation. Costumed and coiffed in character, Mary Beth succeeds in captivating and delighting her audiences with the wit, wisdom, and charm of Mae West while conveying her own entertaining and motivational message.

Gene Griessman captivates audiences with his portrayal of Abraham Lincoln. Arden Bercovitz, as a very believable Albert Einstein, talks about creative thinking and innovation as well as personal and professional development.

Some speakers portray actors and actresses. For example, Carmen D'Amico as Elizabeth Taylor delivers a powerful message about spousal abuse, survival, and self-esteem. Diana Jaffe, a motivational and inspirational speaker, performs in the character of Marilyn Monroe.

Being a character speaker requires a great deal of research and acting ability. Adopting another person's persona means that you must capture and project the essence of that individual, including that person's philosophy and style as well as his or her appearance. A character speaker must skillfully weave actual or paraphrased words spoken by the character into the speaker's motivational or informational message.

Some speakers don costumes to communicate their messages. Bill Stieber illustrates the three social motives of David McClelland's theory on motivation used in leadership training by dressing like three different golfers. After discussing McClelland's theory and behavioral examples of the three social motives, Stieber quizzes the group to guess his primary motive. The first costume he wears is a checkered hat that might be worn by a businessperson and he carries a golf club. He mentions the challenges presented by golfing and the competitiveness it provides. This representation illustrates the need for achievement. The second costume is a funny hat that has an actual golf club and ball as its top. In his monologue, he mentions the opportunity to swap stories with his regular golf buddies and the fun they have in the clubhouse after playing a round of golf. This represents the need for affiliation. Finally, Stieber changes into a sequin-trimmed Army camouflage jacket and dons a camouflage hat. The costume helps him make the point about a person's need for influence, prestige, and power.

One speaker in the health care field, Pam Korte, speaks to nurses on time management. She wears rabbit ears and a rabbit nose, looking like the White Rabbit in *Alice's Adventures in Wonderland,* and rushes into the room with a huge clock yelling, "I'm late! I'm late!" In another session with nurses assigned to geriatric care, Korte enters the room dressed like an elderly woman, complete with wig, glasses, cane, hospital gown, and robe. She is stooped over and has to be helped to the platform by a volunteer participant. In both cases, she has the audience's attention from the very beginning.

When using costumes, it is important that they are easy to put on and remove if you are doing changes on stage. Often, all you need to convey the character is a hat, a wig, a simple piece of clothing, or a prop. Mary Beth Roach recommends using velcro for quick changes and suggests changes should be made in 30 seconds or less. Be very careful that your costume changes don't come across as a "strip show." Try it out on a mixed group of friends and family members who will give you honest feedback.

Characters in the Audience

Sometimes it is effective to "plant" characters in the audience. The key is to ask three or four volunteers ahead of time to play a character related to your topic, such as difficult customers or problem employees. Give each "actor" a one- or two-line script to memorize and explain the cues. In a presentation at an annual international conference sponsored by The American Society for Training and Development, I spoke on the topic "Coping with Classroom Characters, Capers, and Conflict." I had asked three people to portray three difficult participants: the griper, the class clown, and the know-it-all. I began by creating mood by saying, "I'd like you to sit back, think about your experience with conflict, characters, and capers in your classroom. Concentrate very hard. Just maybe, two or three of these characters may come to life. Concentrate . . . concentrate . . . " Just then, my first character, the class clown, complete with a Groucho disguise, jumped from her seat and started telling jokes. I thanked her for her desire to liven up the group and asked her to take her seat so we could get started. Then, my next character, the griper, stood up and began complaining about having to attend an early morning session and remarking about the room being too cold. I acknowledged her concerns, apologized for the early session, and promised we would deal with the temperature situation. Finally, my know-it-all character rose from his seat and proclaimed that he had no idea why he was in this session. After all, he had been a trainer for a year and he was sure he wasn't going to learn anything new from me. I, of course, thanked him for attending and mentioned that I was looking forward to his sharing some of his tips and techniques with us. Although the audience knew this was a staged performance, it immediately drew them in. They were excited and anxious to participate—even at 8:00 A.M. the morning after the conference social.

Creating Characters on the Spot

You don't have to wear a costume to create or portray characters. Great speakers tell stories, and those stories often include more than one person. It's amazing how much more effective your story becomes when you simply change your position on stage and modify your voice to distinguish one character from another. I learned the powerful impact of voice and position at the 1994 NSA Eastern Workshop in Charlotte, North Carolina. I had volunteered to participate in a practicum conducted by the 1996–1997 NSA president, Patricia Ball. Thirteen of us were asked to prepare a three-minute story that we use as part of one of our speeches or presentations. We would tell our stories while 200-plus NSA workshop participants observed, fishbowl style. Patricia would take each of us aside for a brief coaching session, and then we would tell our story again, applying Patricia's tips. I chose the following anecdote, which I use in presentations or seminars on the subject of style differences, how these differences impact communication, and how we need to adjust our styles to improve our interpersonal interaction. This follows an activity in which participants assess their own styles using "The Personality Profile System," by Carlson Learning.

> My husband and I are business partners. I am a very high "D" (Dominant) and he is an "S" (Systematic). He actually runs our business, including all operational aspects such as computer technology. We had decided to purchase a new computer system, and it was his job to decide what we were going to buy. Now, I have to tell you that no matter what we buy, Bob does extensive research, including detailed analyses complete with charts and graphs. So, after several weeks of reading *Consumer Reports* and countless computer publications, he came into my office and announced that he was ready to share his findings. He began by saying, "We could go with option A and it does this, this, and

this. . . . " (I'm giving you the brief executive overview.) "Or we could choose option B and it does this, this, and this. . . . Or, we could go with option C. . . . " At this point, I interrupted and screamed, "I don't care! Just tell me how much it costs, does it do what I want it to do, and when I can have it." At this point, Bob said quietly, "Listen to yourself, oh great communicator. I have a need to explore all options and analyze each one so that we make an informed decision, and you're not allowing me to do that."

He was absolutely right. That incident was a real eye opener for me and really opened our lines of communication. We started talking about our style differences and what we need to do in order to communicate effectively with each other, not only as business partners but also as husband and wife.

Although Patricia's suggestions to me were quite simple, they have made a world of difference when I tell that story. First of all, she suggested that I say, "I'm giving you the brief executive overview," as an aside. Secondly, she told me to turn my body slightly and change my voice when I quoted Bob. In other words, I needed to sound like Bob and indicate through a change of position that I was now speaking as the other person. Next, she encouraged me to scream, "I don't care!" and to lower my voice when I say, "Bob said quietly, 'Listen to yourself, oh great communicator . . . '" Her final coaching tip was for me to pause after I say, "He was absolutely right," as though a light bulb had gone on in my head. When I told the story again using Patricia's suggestions, I was amazed at the difference in the audience's reaction. And the same was true for each of the other practicum participants as they told their stories a second time.

You may also want to adapt a monologue from a play or other genre. For example, to illustrate miscommunication due to misinterpretations of the same word, I adopt the character of Bag Lady Trudy in Jane Wagner's play *The Search for Signs of Intelligent Life in the Universe*, the one-woman show played by Lily Tomlin. Trudy talks about her imaginary space chums. She has the following conversation with herself: "I could kick myself. I told 'em I'd meet 'em on the corner of 'Walk, Don't Walk' 'round lunchtime. Do they even know what 'lunch' means? I doubt it. And 'round'. Why did I say 'round'? Why wasn't I more specific?"

Of course, all your speeches and presentations should be carefully planned and practiced. It's even more critical to rehearse when you are creating characters. Your "production" should be staged very carefully but done in such a way that you come across as believable.

USING MAGIC

You don't have to be a magician to use magic to enhance your speeches, workshops, or seminars. Magic is one of the best visual aids and could have been included in Chapter 4. However, I decided to include it in this chapter because of its theatrical nature.

Magic is a great enhancement. It's fun, has universal appeal, and can be used with any topic. To familiarize yourself with magic tricks and their possible application to your programs, start by visiting magic shops and reading books about the subject. A great resource is *Tricks for Trainers,* by Dave Arch. As you look at and read about magic tricks, brainstorm topics and content points you can illustrate with a particular trick.

Like anything else, using magic will require a lot of practice. Many tricks are easy to learn and even to master, but the challenge to you will be to perform the trick flawlessly. Also, for a magic trick to be effective, it must have a purpose other than to entertain.

DON'T OVERDO

Although we recognize that speaking is a performing art, be careful not to overdo the showmanship. You should use the entertainment factor only to enhance your presentation. When the applause stops and the audience leaves, you want them to remember what you *said*.

6 Creating Word Pictures

We've all heard that a picture is worth a thousand words. What I want to address in this chapter is how words can create a picture. Although audience members are not interacting directly with each other or the speaker, the speaker's ability to use visualization, storytelling, and imagery will greatly enhance the audience's connection with the speaker. In fact, often audience members are so engaged that they feel they are actually part of the speaker's experience.

VISUALIZATION

Visualization is the technique of picturing an object, person, place, or event that is not actually present. The purpose is to help the audience members recall or form a mental image. You must start by creating a mood. Begin by playing some relaxation music, such as a soft classical piece, new age music, or environmental sounds. In smaller groups, I often use an environmental sound machine that allows you to select from a number of sounds, such as a gurgling brook, a summer night, ocean waves, or quiet rain. You can find these mood machines in specialty stores such as the Sharper Image or Brookstone. Then you ask the audience members to close their eyes and breathe deeply and to think about a peaceful place where they like to go. Then you ask series of questions designed to help them visualize or recreate that image in their minds. As you ask questions or give instructions, you should do so slowly and with pauses to allow the images to develop in people's minds. Your voice should be soft and soothing yet loud enough to be heard by everyone in the room.

Visualization can help people become more successful by directing them to use the power of their minds to "see" themselves as successful in a given situation. Athletic coaches often use visualization when coaching players to improve their performance. Instead of having them actually practice shooting the ball into a basketball hoop, the coach will take the team members through a visualization exercise in which they imagine themselves midcourt or at the foul line, throwing the ball and making a perfect shot every time.

For those of you who may be prone to stage fright, here's a visualization exercise for you. Find a comfortable spot, turn on your favorite relaxation music, spend a few moments breathing deeply, and imagine yourself in front of the audience of your dreams. If, for example, you are a business speaker, you see yourself on stage in front of an audience of CEOs from all the Fortune 500 companies. You have already received your fee up front for more than you ever could have hoped for. As you continue to listen to the music and breathe deeply, visualize the following:

- What are you wearing? (It should be something in which you feel and look great.)
- What time of day is it?
- What does the room look like?
- What kind of lighting do you have?
- What are you talking about?

Next, imagine that every person in the audience is hanging on your every word. You are calm and confident as you deliver your perfect presentation. The audience members laugh at your humor, nod their heads in agreement, and clap with thunderous applause during a standing ovation at the conclusion of your talk. You are elated and experience an adrenaline high as audience members approach you with words of praise. How do you feel now? The next time you experience anxiety and nervousness before a speech, presentation, or seminar, take a few moments to visualize your moment of glory and the feeling of success you experienced. You'll be amazed at the powerful impact it has on reducing your fear and stress.

Creating Scenarios

In a visualization variation, I asked an audience of trainers at a conference to picture themselves in the following scenario:

> You're sitting in your office reflecting on the feedback received several months after completion of a comprehensive, costly, and what you thought was a successful customer service training program. Yet now, months later, nothing's changed. Employees apparently aren't using what they learned. Customer complaints are at an all-time high, line managers are complaining that the training was a waste of time, and senior management is questioning the amount of money spent on the program and pressuring you to do something about it. You ask yourself, "What happened? What went wrong? What can I do about it?" Can anyone identify with this scenario?

After acknowledging the nodding of heads in agreement, I went on to introduce my topic by stating that lack of management involvement and reinforcement back on the job were often why training doesn't work. I created a scenario with which probably everyone in the room could identify. I asked them to imagine themselves in that situation. Once again, they were immediately engaged because I created a word picture in which they could place themselves.

As another example, I opened a concurrent session by asking the following rhetorical question: "Does it seem to you
that a lot of people and organizations talk a lot about quality
service but that nobody seems to be doing anything about it?"
(Pause) "Do any of the following scenarios sound familiar?"

Scene 1—One employee to another
"I'm getting pretty fed up with this place. They pay us
next to nothing and treat us like dirt. Then they expect
us to be nice to the customers. Why should we?"

Scene 2—One manager to another
"I just don't understand today's employees. They don't
care about anything except themselves. We've spent a
lot of money on a customer service training program
and yet the number of customer complaints and
employee errors is as high as ever. We should just fire
them all and start over with people who really want to
work."

Scene 3—One person to another in an airport waiting area
"It's the same everywhere you go—banks, department
stores, restaurants, airports. The service is lousy. Companies don't care about quality service. The people waiting
on you act like they're doing you a favor. They're unre-
sponsive, incompetent, and rude."

I continued by asking, "Do any of these scenes sound familiar?
Scenes like these are repeated daily throughout the country as
service providers and consumers struggle with the quality service dilemma. So what are we going to do about it?" I then
offered my strategies for creating a customer-focused culture.

STORYTELLING

What exactly is storytelling? In *Using Stories and Humor—Grab
Your Audience* (another book in *The Essence of Public Speaking*

Series), author Joanna Slan defines storytelling, citing Norma J. Livo and Sandra A. Rietz, authors of *Storytelling Process and Practice*. According to Livo and Rietz, "Storytelling is an oral art form whose practice provides a means of preserving and transmitting images, ideas, motivations, and emotions that are universal across human communities." Storytelling has been used to captivate audiences throughout the ages. It's an art as old as mankind. Throughout history, stories have passed from generation to generation as a means of preserving a group's culture, heritage, history, and tradition. Stories teach a lesson as well as entertain. Stories are at the very heart of who we are as human beings. Our first exposure to stories was as children listening to bedtime stories told by our parents. As we grew up, we continued to hear stories from teachers telling us about famous people in history, religious leaders teaching us valuable life lessons through Bible stories, and family members regaling us with stories of their own childhood adventures. Stories touch us in a way that no other medium can. Stories reach in and grab at the core of our existence. They help define who we are and what we believe. It is just as powerful, and perhaps even more so, today as it was a thousand years ago. Throughout the world, every culture has its own oral history. The ancient Greeks, Romans, and Vikings as well as the American Indians are rich in folklore. Explore the world of ancient storytelling and you will discover the reasons the best speakers use stories so extensively and successfully in their presentations.

Special Types of Stories

Parables

Parables are short narratives from which a moral can be drawn. One of the most familiar sources of parables is the Bible. Example: The prodigal sun who squanders all his money but returns home to a forgiving father.

Fables

Fables are brief tales from folklore, sometimes using animals that speak and act as humans. *Aesop's Fables* is probably the best-known collection of fables. These charming and simple tales teach valuable and timeless life lessons. Example: "The Crab and Its Mother" teaches a lesson about the power of example. In this fable, the mother crab chastises her son for walking one-sided instead of straight forward. The young crab agrees to do so if his mother can show him how. The mother tries and tries but cannot model the behavior she expects from her son.

Spend some time reading parables, fables, myths, and even fairy tales. Think about how you can use existing ones in your presentations to reinforce your message. Better still, try your hand at making up your own tales to drive home a point.

Telling Personal Stories

The best speakers are master storytellers. I discovered the power of storytelling quite by accident. I never planned on using stories—they just happened. I began using stories in my training sessions to illustrate or further explain my learning points. Several years ago, I began asking participants at the end of a session, "What did you like best about this program?" The response is always the same. Participants always say they like two things: the activities and the stories. One day I decided to ask what they liked about the stories. As one participant put it, "They made the ideas and points come alive. We could really relate to your experiences."

One of my favorite and crowd-pleasing stories is used to illustrate differences in personality and communication styles. I distribute and ask participants to complete a self-assessment personality profile. (The one I use most frequently is the *Personality Profile System,* by Carlson Learning.) I then put people into groups according to their preferred styles and ask each group to make a list of how it would like to learn how to drive a stick-shift car. I also ask them to put their lists on flip-chart pages and to post them on the wall. The lists are quite interesting and generally break down as follows:

■ **Dominant.** Their list is quite short and reflects an action orientation. Basically, their method is: "Give me the keys, give me the car, and get out of my way!"

■ **Influencing.** The influencers' list is somewhat similar to that of the dominant group. The influencing group, however, reflects a social orientation. Several items on the list refer to people in some way. The list is also not in any particular order. Sometimes this group will also include the specific car they want to drive (generally a sports car).

■ **Systematic.** The systematic folks present a very detailed and numbered list, reflecting their logical, analytical nature. Their list includes reading the manual and wanting to understand clearly how the gears and clutch work.

■ **Conscientious.** The conscientious group is somewhat similar to the systematic group in that its list is numbered and also reflects a step-by-step process. This list, however, includes the element of caution. The conscientious group wants plenty of opportunities to practice in a parking lot before going into traffic, and it wants to be taught by a patient instructor.

Following the comparison of the lists, I conduct a discussion of how these differences play out in both our personal and professional lives. I then tell the story about the style differences between my husband and me that I recounted in Chapter 5.

That story always gets a laugh, especially after I incorporated Patricia Ball's coaching suggestions. I then go on to ask the participants how they think he should have approached me, and if the situation were reversed, how I should communicate with him if I want his cooperation and buy-in. The story really helps clarify the role communication and personality styles play in relationships. For many, it's like turning on a light bulb for them. In every group, I have at least one person who tells me either in the session or at break, "Now I understand why my husband (boss, sister, friend, mother, etc.) and I have such a difficult time communicating."

Why Storytelling Works

Storytelling engages the individual audience members, allowing them to relate to or identify with the speaker's story. They have either had a similar experience or they are reminded of a similar situation that evoked the same thoughts, feelings, or reaction. Storytelling forms a psychological bond with the audience because it describes a common human experience.

New speakers, in particular, will ask, "Where do I get my stories and how many stories should I tell?" Let's address the second half of the question first. Some speakers recommend that you tell three stories per hour. Others say you should punctuate every main learning point with a story. How many and when really depends on personal preference and style.

The answer to the first part of the question is much simpler. Tell your own stories. Our life experiences provide a wealth of stories from the humorous to the poignant. When we use stories from our own lives, the emotion is real, and that authenticity comes across to your audience. Some speakers will use stories from other sources. *Reader's Digest,* in particular, seems to be a popular source. The danger here is not only that the genuine emotion is absent but also that many people may have already heard or read the story. Your credibility is at risk. For example, in his book *Seven Habits of Highly Effective People,* Stephen Covey retells a story told by Frank Koch in *Proceedings,* the magazine of the Naval Institute.*

---

*Reprinted from *Procceedings* with permission; Copyright © (1987) U.S. Naval Institute.

Two battleships assigned to the training squadron had been at sea on maneuvers in heavy weather for several days. I was serving on the lead battleship and was on watch on the bridge as night fell. The visibility was poor with patchy fog, so the captain remained on the bridge keeping an eye on all activities.

Shortly after dark, the lookout on the wing of the bridge reported, "Light, bearing on the starboard bow."

"Is it steady or moving astern?" the captain called out.

Lookout replied, "Steady, captain," which meant we were on a dangerous collision course with that ship.

The captain then called to the signal man, "Signal that ship: We are on a collision course, advise you change course 20 degrees."

Back came a signal, "Advisable for you to change course 20 degrees."

The captain said, "Send, I'm a captain, change course 20 degrees."

"I'm a seaman second class," came the reply. "You had better change course 20 degrees."

By that time, the captain was furious. He spat out, "Send, I'm a battleship. Change course 20 degrees."

Back came the flashing light, "I'm a lighthouse."

We changed course.

That's a great story and obviously a lot of other speakers think it is, too. If I hear that story told one more time, I think I'll scream. Not only has it lost its impact on an audience, but also the speaker who tells it also loses his or her credibility.

One source of stories that is absolutely, positively off limits is another speaker. Many speakers are known for their "signature" stories; that is, personal stories unique to them that serve as a cornerstone for many of their speeches and presentations. Jeanne Robertson's baton story, Grady Jim Robinson's basketball story, among others—they are all examples of stories identified with one particular speaker. Unfortunately, other speakers will hear the story and then incorporate it into their own material without crediting the speaker who owns it. Many of these well-known keynote speakers have told of having a preceding speaker use the keynoter's story or joke as his or her own, leaving the real pro to switch gears at the last minute. Using another speaker's story and passing it off as your own is stealing, plain and simple!

To help you develop your own unique signature stories, begin keeping a journal. Capture your stories right after the events occur. Be as detailed as possible; you can always tighten it later. In addition to recording the events, note your (or others') reaction to the situation and jot down the message or learning point. I will even jot down possible topics where I think the story might fit. The same story, of course, can be used in different contexts as well as used to illustrate different points. Joel Weldon advises speakers to relate "each point of your story to the audience so as to meet a need, overcome a fear, and reinforce a victory."

Inappropriate Stories

Just like visual aids and activities, stories must be planned very carefully, taking into account factors such as the makeup of the audience, the occasion, type of business, and your purpose. To illustrate my point about the importance of taking a systems approach to customer service, I tell the following story:

> I was in the mall one day buying a few new outfits before going to a conference. I headed for one of the major department stores on the East Coast. Pressed for time, I quickly grabbed several items from the racks and raced into the fitting room. I was stopped in my tracks by an unfriendly attendant who yelled, "Hold it!" and pointed to the sign that read, "Only 3 Items Are Permitted in the Dressing Rooms." I knew, of

course, I was a bit over my limit, but I explained that I was in a hurry and I would bring out the same number of items I took in. She abruptly told me that it was store policy and there were no exceptions. I responded that I understood she was just doing her job but suggested that she pass on to the "powers above" that if the retailers want people to buy merchandise, then they should make it easy to do so. About that time, a sales associate came by. Overhearing part of the conversation, she demanded to know what my problem was. I repeated my suggestion but was stopped short by the sales associate: "We don't make the policy. We just enforce it!" At that point, I put down my items, went to the competitor at the other end of the mall, and bought the same merchandise I had intended to try on in the first place.

In contrast, a week later I once again found myself in a store in another state and a similar scenario of having more items to try on than are "permitted" in the dressing room. This time the situation was different. This time the sales associate said, "Oh, that's okay. I see you have four items instead of three. And if you need another size or color, just yell and I'll be happy to get it for you." I was determined not to leave the store without buying something because the sales associate made me want to buy by creating a positive environment.

I go on to say that the security policy and procedure was not customer friendly. And all the customer service training in the world will be useless if an organization's delivery systems, security systems, etc., do not support and reflect a customer-focused orientation.

This story probably would not be appropriate with an all-male audience. I could, however, modify the story to make it less female-oriented by substituting a product with more general application. This practice of modifying a story brings up the issue of absolute truth versus poetic license. We do not have to tell a story *exactly* as it happened. After all, our purpose in telling it is to capture the essence of its life lesson as a way to reinforce our message.

Another consideration in terms of appropriateness is using the name of a specific business or organization. Since my story reflected negatively on the famous retailer, it would have been extremely inappropriate for me to mention the name of the department store. Not only is it unprofessional, it is also potentially libelous. Positive stories, of course, are almost always welcomed by an organization. Even then, there are some exceptions. One of my clients, a prominent investment banking firm, does not permit vendors, consultants, speakers, etc., to acknowledge publicly their relationship with the firm. So before you use the name of an organization in your presentation, make sure there are no possible repercussions.

Storytelling can be planned or spontaneous. Generally speaking, the shorter the presentation, the more carefully you must plan where and how you are going to use your story. In longer programs such as workshops or seminars, you may find yourself spontaneously pulling out an appropriate story from your "story bag" to further clarify your learning point.

Story Structure

A good story doesn't just happen. It takes thought, planning, and structure. Most literary genres follow a similar structural pattern of development:

- ■ **Exposition**
  This is the presentation of essential information, including the setting and characters.

- ■ **Complication**
  As the story unfolds, the teller or writer creates interest and tension by introducing a complication, problem, or conflict; also known as rising action.

▪ Climax

The climax is the high point or turning point of the story. It is the moment in which tension is high.

▪ Resolution

In literary terms, the resolution is also called dénouement. Here the character experiences a recognition, disclosure, or discovery; also known as falling action.

▪ Conclusion

This is the moral of the story. In other words, this is what you want the audience to take from the experience.

To understand better how this structure plays out, let's take a look once again at my story about style differences and see how the story follows this pattern of development:

▪ Exposition

"My husband and I are business partners. I am a very high "D" (Dominant) and he is an "S" (Systematic). He actually runs our business, including all operational aspects such as computer technology. We had decided to purchase a new computer system, and it was his job to decide what we were going to buy.

▪ Complication

"Now, I have to tell you that no matter what we buy, Bob does extensive research, including detailed analyses complete with charts and graphs. So, after several weeks of reading *Consumer Reports* and countless computer publications, he came into my office and announced that he was ready to share his findings. He began by saying, 'We could go with option A and it does this, this, and this . . .' (I'm giving you the brief executive overview.) 'Or we could choose option B and it does this, this, and this. . . . Or, we could go with option C. . . .'

▪ Climax

"At this point, I interrupted and screamed, 'I don't care! Just tell me how much it costs, does it do what I want it to do, and when I can have it.' At this point, Bob said quietly, 'Listen to yourself, oh great communicator. I have a need to explore all options and analyze each one so that we make an informed decision, and you're not allowing me to do that.'

■ **Resolution**

"He was absolutely right. That incident was a real eye opener for me and really opened our lines of communication.

■ **Conclusion**

"We started talking about our style differences and what we need to do in order to communicate effectively with each other, not only as business partners but also as husband and wife."

WORD POWER

Have you ever known someone who seemed to be a master of "turning a phrase"? While it's true that some people seem to have a natural flair for words, you, too, can learn to use colorful language to make your presentations come alive.

Rhyming

What about rhyming in speaking? Rhymes are very much a part of our lives. One of the first learning exercises we ever did as children was to learn nursery rhymes:

> Hickory, dickory, dock!
> The mouse ran up the clock;
> The clock struck one,
> The mouse ran down,
> Hickory, dickory, dock!

As we grew older, the subjects changed but the rhyming remained:

Roses are red,
Violets are blue,
Sugar is sweet,
And so are you.

Even today, newsmakers around the world are making their words impactful and unforgettable by using rhymes. For example, during the O.J. Simpson criminal trial, defense attorney Johnnie Cochran made a powerful plea to the jury by saying, "If it doesn't fit, you must acquit," in reference to the black leather glove that appeared not to fit Simpson's hand. In another example, critics of big business and corruption in corporate America have warned, "Crime in the suites is worse than crime in the streets." Rhyming works because it makes ideas easy to remember and is pleasing to the ear.

Imagery

Imagery is the use of words to create pictures in the minds of the audience. Good speakers draw the picture very carefully so that audiences can share the speaker's experience and remember the speaker's message. One of the most masterful people in creating imagery is 1994–1995 NSA president Naomi Rhode. Naomi's soft, soothing tone and her ability to create vivid word pictures are a powerful combination. To listen to her is to be mesmerized and transported to another time and place. For those brief moments, we see the beautiful hues of a tropical sunset, hear the wind blowing through the trees, or feel the warm sun on our faces.

There are a number of ways to create imagery. To help you better understand these techniques, let's look at their definitions and examples.

Metaphors

Metaphors compare unlike things. Example: I use sailing as a metaphor for the stages of team development. Setting sail represents the forming stage; rough seas, storming; dead in the water, norming; and smooth sailing, performing.

Simile

Similes make explicit comparisons between unlike things using the words *like, as,* or *is.* Example: He is like a fish out of water.

Analogies

Analogies compare something complex to something ordinary and familiar. Example: NSA member Bill Ringle provides training on computer technology, calling it "driver's education for the information superhighway."

Epithets

Epithets are words or phrases expressing a characteristic of someone or something. Example: Richard the Lionhearted or the Cowardly Lion from *The Wizard of Oz.* Sometimes the characterizing word or phrase associated with the person or thing is used in place of it. Example: "man's best friend" is an epithet for dog.

Personification

Personification is the attribution of human characteristics to nonhuman or inanimate objects or to abstract ideas. Example: Here's an excerpt from "I Am Your Flag," by Bob Nelson of KYW Newsradio 1060 in Philadelphia.

Traditionalists say I was born of a woman's hand . . . fashioned from bits of colored cloth by a seamstress in a small house in Philadelphia, a year after the new country was born.

Historians are less certain of my origin. Yet, no one doubts my existence. I was created out of necessity to serve as the emblem of a people whose experiment in nationhood was as unique as the arrangement of my Stars and Stripes. . . .

I was created to serve a people in struggle and a government in change. There are now more stars in my blue field than there were in the beginning and, if need be, there's room for more.

But those red and white stripes remain as they've always remained, clearly visible through the struggle . . . the symbol of the "land of the free and the home of the brave."

I am your past. I am your future. I am your flag!*

According to Patricia Fripp in her article in the March 1994 issue of *Professional Speaker*, "Audiences don't remember what we say; they remember the pictures we create in their minds." People will remember the stories and metaphors long after the facts are forgotten.

Choose two or three imagery techniques and try to use them in your next speech or presentation.

HUMOR

Many speakers balk at the idea of using humor in their presentations or seminars. They argue that they are not humorists, and some even go so far as to say that they do not use humor because learning is serious business. First, let's distinguish between humorists and humorous speakers. A

---

*Reprinted courtesy KYW Newsradio.

humorist focuses primarily on entertainment with some content. The humorist's presentation is based on stories and social commentaries having a humorous twist. On the other hand, a humorous speaker is content-focused, using humorous stories and comments to add the entertainment factor. Any speaker can be humorous.

Reasons to Use Humor

Makes the Audience Feel Good

As NSA member Stephen Tweed once told me, "People want to feel good and have their problems solved, in that order." After all, we're there to meet the audience's needs.

Makes Your Content More Memorable

People are much more likely to remember your points if they can associate them with something humorous you have done or said.

Helps You Connect with the Audience

Humor is a basic element of the human condition. It creates an instant bond because you have all shared a common emotional experience.

Makes You Seem More Real and Human

Humor is a great leveler or equalizer. Because you allow some of your realness to show through, the audience will be more accepting of what you have to say. It will see you as "one of us" instead of some pontificating, self-proclaimed guru telling people how they should live their lives.

Helps Illustrate Important Points

Sometimes what may seem perfectly clear to us just doesn't compute with the audience. Humor helps bridge that gap and presents the information in a more easily understood way.

Creates a Positive Environment

If people are laughing and enjoying themselves, it disarms them. Even the most negative, pessimistic, and skeptical person will find himself or herself more receptive to your message.

Keeps People's Attention

When humor is used, people will pay more attention because they don't want to miss anything or feel left out. Think about how uncomfortable you are when everyone around you is laughing at something the speaker said and you missed it because you were busy thinking about or doing something else.

Gets You More Business

Some speakers will ask the pros, "Do I have to use humor?" The common response is: "No, you don't have to use humor, unless you want to get paid." Let's be candid. Humor sells. So if you want to be a successful speaker, make it a point to include humor in every presentation you make. Even extremely serious topics require the occasional light touch.

Using One Liners

Some speakers prepare a list of one liners or ad libs that they appear to use spontaneously when something goes wrong in the middle of their presentations. We've all experienced these disasters: you drop something, the power goes off, the equipment doesn't work, the microphone squeals, the group in the next room is making too much noise, the fire alarm goes off, your materials don't arrive—the list is endless. If you are prepared to say something witty when disaster strikes, you will minimize your own anxiety and come across as the polished professional you are. There are two ways you can come up with appropriate one liners. First, develop your own. Start by keeping a list of the things that go wrong or that you imagine could go wrong. Then jot down an appropriate witty remark to deal with each one. For those of us who are not so quick-witted, seek out sources of prepared oneliners. NSA member Tom Antion has put together an eight-page booklet of great ad libs for almost any situation.

Sources of Humor

Your Experiences

Your own life is a great source of humorous happenings. Professional speaker and retired professor Lyle Crist entertains and enlightens his audiences by using humorous stories and anecdotes drawn from his long tenure as an English professor at Mount Union College. Keep a list of funny things that happen to you or humorous remarks you make. We often say something humorous quite unintentionally and are surprised that it gets a laugh. When you get such a response from an audience or even a group of friends, write it down. You never know where and when you might be able to use it. Here's where taping your speech or presentation can be helpful. You can listen to your tape and track the audience's response, not-ing uproarious laughter versus polite chuckling.

Don't be afraid to make fun of yourself. Audiences love self-deprecating humor. It gives them a chance to see you as a human being who does dumb things and makes silly mis-takes—just like them.

Other People's Experiences

Friends, colleagues, and family members often will share their own humorous anecdotes. Sometimes, when you hear other people's stories, you say to yourself, "What a great story. I wish that had happened to me. It would be perfect for my speech on . . . " Don't be afraid to use other people's stories, but be sure to ask their permission and give the appropriate attribution when telling it. Who knows? They may even give you the right to use it as your own.

Books on Humor

No speaker's library should be without at least one book on humor. There are plenty of books, articles, and newsletters that deal with humor of all types and for any occasion.

News Stories, Headlines, and Advertisements

If you have any doubt about how outrageously funny these can be, watch Jay Leno on Monday nights. He does a segment in which he just reads humorous headlines, advertising slogans, and news clips that his viewers send in. Real-life gaffes often provide the most amusing examples of human foibles and folly.

Product Labels

Early in the summer, our kitchen was plagued with a major ant problem. Because we have two cats, we were concerned about using a pesticide spray. As an alternative, I bought ant traps. You know, they're those little white "houses" with multiple entrances. Ants are supposed to go in them, magically gather poison dust, and carry the toxic substance back to their nest. Guess what? It didn't work! We watched as dozens and dozens of ants walked around and over the traps but never went in. The problem became intolerable, so my husband set out to find a spray that would be safe for pets. After reading every label of every bug-killer spray on the shelf, he came home with a "safe" spray. Of course, I had to read the label myself—just to be sure. I burst into laughter as I read the list of pests exterminated by the insect killer: "ants, bedbugs, carpet beetles, centipedes, cheese mites, clothes moths, cockroaches, *confused flour beetles . . .* " I couldn't read any further. For some reason, I was struck by the image of a beetle walking around in a stupor. My husband, on the other hand, couldn't see anything humorous about a confused flour beetle. (I would love to know what one looks like.) I have no idea how I'm going to use that story, but I'm sure I will.

Cartoons and Comic Strips

When something tickles your funny bone, write it down. Most likely, your audiences will find it funny, too. One of my favorites is a *Family Circus* cartoon showing a mother opening the front door. On the other side of the threshold is her little boy with a huge bunch of other children behind him. The caption reads: "You said I could bring some friends home with me, but I don't know how many 'some' is." I show this cartoon in a variety of programs to reinforce my message about different interpretations of the same word.

In a session on motivation, I use a cartoon depicting Noah and his ark. The accompanying words represent the voice of God saying, "Motivation? You want motivation? I'm going to put this planet under 200 feet of water, you twit!"

Dilbert, by Scott Adams, is particularly popular right now with business audiences. The cartoon satirizes corporate America. Showing the absurdity of today's workplace helps ease the pain for many who have fallen victim to restructuring, downsizing, reengineering, and the like. Instead of gloom and doom, people learn to laugh at themselves, their situations, and each other, proving once again that humor is the best medicine.

Radio and Television

Situation comedies are great sources of humor. You can relate a vignette you saw on TV even if the audience isn't familiar with the show and the characters. Just be sure to provide the appropriate amount of background information so the audience understands the context.

To help you become more skilled at and comfortable with using humor in your presentations, watch and listen to the masters. If you're a member of NSA, buy NSA tapes of sessions delivered by humorists or join the NSA Humor PEG (Professional Emphasis Group). Watch comedians such as Jay Leno and David Letterman, or buy tapes or CDs recorded by other well-known comedians. Watch and listen carefully to what they do that gets the audience laughing. Write it down and review it when you prepare for your next keynote or presentation. The more you can expose yourself to humor, the more your creative juices will flow. You might be surprised to learn how naturally funny and witty you are.

7

Audience Participation

Today's audiences want to be involved; they are no longer content just to sit there and listen to a speaker. They want to learn, and they want to be involved in the learning process. When people are involved, they are physically or mentally engaged in what is going on at that moment. Involvement can take many forms: visual, physical, verbal, emotional, mental, and spiritual. It is up to us as speakers to actively engage the audience by appealing to one or more of these states.

Based on hundreds of studies on learning, and on the adult learner in particular, we know that learning is more effective when people have an opportunity to learn from each other in pairs or in small groups. We also know that adult learners want concrete examples that they can relate to. Furthermore, as we noted earlier, interactive computers, multimedia, and a multitude of high-tech, immediate response gadgetry have conditioned today's audiences. The challenge to us speakers is to get them involved while maintaining control. In a keynote or conference breakout session, one of the dangers of audience involvement is that audience members can easily run away with the session. As with anything else in speaking, it's all in the technique. Planning is critical. In preparing for audience involvement and interaction, be sure to allow adequate time, keeping in mind that activities, and particularly answers to questions initiated by the speaker, usually take longer than planned. One way of exercising a degree of control is to set ground rules and guidelines, such as time limits for each person's response. Remember that when you add audience involvement and interaction, you must decrease the amount of information you can disseminate. What you lose in content, however, you will gain in audience enjoyment of the experience and retention of and ability to use the material you did cover.

REASONS FOR AUDIENCE INVOLVEMENT

Before we get into specific techniques, let's look at the benefits of involving your audience in your speech, presentation, or training session.

- **Establish rapport.** People who are involved have a much warmer, more receptive attitude toward you.
- **Reinforce key points.** Involvement techniques help increase the retention of your message. As noted earlier, studies show us that people retain approximately 15 percent of what they hear. When visuals are added, the retention rate increases to around 55 percent. Amazingly, when people have a chance to hear, see, and *do,* they retain up to 80 percent.
- **Gather information about the audience.** The more opportunities you give participants to be active and involved, the more you will find out about them through both direct observation and the use of specific activities aimed at culling specific information.
- **Gain and maintain the audience's attention.** People have short attention spans, and involvement techniques will increase their focus and concentration.
- **Energize the group.** It's difficult for any of us to sit for any length of time and still maintain a high energy level.
- **Provide entertainment.** The entertainment factor cannot be overlooked. The more people enjoy the experience, the more they are likely to learn.

There is a saying: "The mind can absorb to the degree the 'bottom' can endure." In general, 90 minutes is the length of time people are willing to sit. Out of those 90 minutes, people will be "with you" for 20 minutes, and those 20 minutes will be different for each person. With that in mind, a good rule of thumb is to change your method of delivery every 8 to 10 minutes at most.

Mikki Williams recommends that you should have your audience doing something active, such as raising hands or writing something down, every 5 to 7 minutes. She suggests that speakers make a list of interactive ideas and then, like a chef using herbs and spices to enhance the flavor of a dish he or she is preparing, the speaker will "sprinkle the activities throughout the speech, presentation, seminar, or workshop."

FORMULA FOR SUCCESS

Audiences are sophisticated, and for that reason, they don't fall for cheap gimmicks. It is important, therefore, to make sure that your method or activity has a purpose. It must relate to the content of your presentation. Also, it must follow a simple three-step formula if it is to be effective in reinforcing the point you are trying to convey. The amount of time spent on each step depends on the length and complexity of the activity.

- **Introduce the activity.** First, you must introduce the activity. To introduce the activity, explain exactly what you want audience members to do. Provide whatever background information they may need, and in some situations, give an example or model of what you want them to do.
- **Conduct the activity.** As people are working in groups, be sure to walk around to clarify instructions as necessary and to keep them on track.

- **Process the activity.** Processing an activity involves discussing what audience members experienced while they were doing the activity, what learning they gleaned, and how they might apply it to their own situation. Every activity must be processed. We cannot assume that participants will be able to draw the parallels and meanings from the activity to their own situation. Many speakers and trainers make a serious mistake by engaging participants in an activity and then moving on without any discussion as to the meaning and purpose of the exercise.

CHOOSING APPROPRIATE ACTIVITIES

Many factors should be taken into consideration when choosing an activity.

- **Size of audience.** Some activities are more effective with small groups, others are more appropriate for large groups, and some can be used regardless of group size.
- **Demographic makeup of the audience.** This is the age of diversity, and that means that audiences are made up of people from many different cultures and backgrounds. Cultural differences, hygiene factors, and personal preference all play a part in determining what activities you should and should not use. Some can cause more harm than good. Consider the following activities and think about how people might react to them.

Shoulder Massage

Speakers and trainers often use this popular activity as an energizer in the middle of a long program. The speaker asks participants to stand and turn to their left. Then the speaker tells them to put their arms on the shoulders of the person in front of them and to give that person a shoulder massage. After a minute or two, the speaker asks them to turn 180 degrees and do the same to the person on their right. How would you react? Some people really enjoy it; they love having their shoulders massaged and loosening those tense muscles. Others are completely turned off and extremely uncomfortable about having a stranger or casual acquaintance be so close and so intimate. We must consider that many people do not like to be touched, as a result of either their cultural background or a personal idiosyncrasy. Their negative reaction to the activity is likely to become a negative reaction to the speaker. Only you can determine if it's worth the risk.

Shoe Exchange

Another questionable activity is the "Shoe Exchange." This is an experiential method of illustrating the concept of "putting yourself in another person's shoes." The speaker asks the audience members to take off their shoes. Then the speaker tells them to exchange shoes with the person next to them and to put the other person's shoes on their feet. Of course, being in the other person's shoes feels awkward and uncomfortable and makes an interesting point. Some people, however, may react negatively. Some may not like the idea of putting their feet in someone else's smelly, sweaty shoes. Others may be annoyed at the possibility of having their expensive shoes stretched out of shape by someone with a larger shoe size. Once again, whether to use the activity is a judgment call.

■ **Room Setup.** Although you should not be constrained by the physical setup of the environment, the reality is that it can sometimes be very restrictive. For example, if you are in a very confined space, activities that require a great deal of movement should be kept to a minimum. In those cases, you will probably need to rely on group activities that involve seat partners rather than to break into small groups.

■ **Time available.** Some activities require more time than others. You must, therefore, decide how you are going to incorporate activities without sacrificing content. In a keynote or breakout session, you will be forced to use fewer activities and those that take only a few minutes. Lengthy role plays, case studies, and simulations would not be appropriate.

■ **Your purpose.** In planning your speech, presentation, workshop, or seminar, be very clear with yourself about what you want to accomplish. Think about that purpose in terms of what you want the audience members to be able to do with the information you are giving them. Determine your key learning points and then choose activities that will illustrate or reinforce your points. It's very important that you don't just insert an activity for the sake of an activity. It must have a purpose.

The following are some audience involvement activities that work well in any size group. I have used these techniques with audiences ranging in size from 15 to 800. Obviously, the larger the group, the more thought must go into the preparation and logistics.

GET THEM ACTIVE FROM THE START

Immediate involvement techniques are very effective in engaging your audience members, piquing their interest and curiosity, and getting them ready to receive your message. Some say we have 20 seconds to grab the audience's attention. If that's true, then we had better make it quick and make it good.

Human Scavenger Hunt

In programs of three hours or more, you may want participants to get to know each other quickly so you can establish a

safe environment in which people will feel comfortable participating. One of the most popular get-acquainted activities that
also guarantees instant involvement is the "Human Scavenger
Hunt," which can be found in *Games Trainers Play,* by Ed
Scannell and John Newstrom. Prepare a sheet on which you
ask participants to "find someone in your group who . . . "
and then list a number of descriptive statements. Ask participants to circulate around the room and to find people who fit
those criteria. When a person fits a particular criterion, ask
that person to sign his or her name. Remind them that an
individual can sign another person's sheet only once. The following scavenger hunt might be used for a financial services
management development session;

Find someone in this group who . . .

- Has more than two pets _____

- Has been a manager/supervisor for more than three years

  _____

- Has the same first initial as you _____

- Has the same number of brothers or sisters as you do ____

  _____

- Has traveled more than 90 miles to get here _____

  _____

- Has been a manager/supervisor for less than one year ____

  _____

- Enjoys attending seminars and workshops _____

  _____

- Is active in a professional or civic organization _____

  _____

- Has survived a merger or downsizing _____

- Is a bank officer _____

- Has worked for more than one financial services organization _____

- Directly manages or supervises more than five people ____
_____

Notice that the statements are both content-related and personal. That gives people an opportunity to relate on a personal level while preparing them mentally for the session content.

The Party

This activity is great for networking and getting acquainted. It creates movement and enables people to meet a number of fellow participants, regardless of the group size. The topics discussed can be adapted to any content.

1. Prior to the activity, hang or display posters on the wall or on easels around the room. The posters should be related to both the theme of your session and your topic. For example, you could use movie posters for a movie theme in a session on conflict, leadership, communication—almost any subject. To make the theme more specific, you could have a specific type or category of movies, such as Disney films, science fiction, horror, westerns, musicals, comedies—the possibilities are endless. For a zoo theme in a diversity program, post large pictures of different zoo animals. Posters representing different sports (football, tennis, golf, basketball, soccer, hockey, skating, etc.) or perhaps teams within a particular sport would be great for adapting a sports theme to team building.

2. Tell participants that they are to look around the room at the posters and to select their three favorites. Explain that

there will be three rounds of groupings or gatherings. During the first round, they are to go to the designated area for their first choice; during the second round, for their second choice; during the third round, for their third choice. You will also tell them how long they will have for each round.

3. Once the subgroups are formed, ask the participants to discuss the questions or topics that appear on their instruction sheet for each round. You could also post the questions on a flip-chart page or transparency before the beginning of each round. The following are sample rounds:

    Round #1 • Please introduce yourself to your group members by stating your name, where you live, and your position and responsibilities.

    • Also explain briefly why you selected this particular (movie, animal, sport, etc.) as your favorite.

    Round #2 • Identify something you have in common with the other members in your group. Some possible topics might include hobbies, sports activities, family, pets, job, etc.

    Round #3 • What are your concerns or expectations for his session?

4. After each round, the facilitator will process the activity by selecting participants at random to respond to the following questions:

    Round #1 • Who in your group traveled the farthest?

    • Why did you choose this (movie, sport, team, etc.)?

    Round #2 • What did you find you have in common?

    Round #3 • What were the major concerns or expectations in your group?

    • What was the most interesting thing you learned through this activity?

This activity can also be used at any time during the session by making the questions content specific. For example, in a change management program, you might ask the following:

Round #1 • What changes are you experiencing in your organization?

Round #2 • What is the impact of change on employees?

Round #3 • What is the impact of change on you as a manager?

Active Knowledge Sharing

Often, speakers begin by citing some interesting facts or statistical information. Audience members' reactions can range from genuine interest to polite attention to eyes glazing over. Rather than giving them the facts and figures, you can use a method called "Active Knowledge Sharing" from *101 Ways to Make Training Active* by Mel Silberman and Karen Lawson. Ask participants to work together in twos or threes and to make an educated guess. You would then show a prepared slide, transparency, or computer screen on which you have provided the factual statement with the number or percentage to be filled in by the participants.

For a session on customer service, you might use the following facts to spur curiosity:

1. _____ percent of the customers will never tell you about a problem; they just go elsewhere.
2. The average customer tells _____ to _____ other people about the problem.
3. One of the primary reasons customers leave is due to an attitude of _____.
4. Customer service is the third most stressful occupation after _____ and _____.

Answers: 1. 96; 2. 9 to 10; 3. indifference; 4. air traffic controller and police officer

If it is a small group (20 to 25), I will go around the room and ask people to give me their figures quickly, which I write on a flip chart or on the overhead. If the group is large, I will ask a few people at random to share their figures. I then show the correct information. Audiences really enjoy this activity. It takes very little time, yet it piques their interest and curiosity. They are motivated to listen because they want to find out if they were correct. It is important to have them work with at least one other person because it doesn't put the individual on the spot. It creates a safe environment for the audience members. People are much more likely to remember these facts and figures because they were directly involved.

Instant Assessment

Another activity from *101 Ways to Make Training Active* that gets people involved right from the beginning is called an "Instant Assessment." Prior to the session, I prepare sets of four different colored 3 x 5 cards, each with a large letter *A*, *B*, *C*, or *D* on it. Each audience member receives a set of cards. I begin the presentation by telling them that I like to find out a little more about them so I can address their specific needs. I then tell them that I am going to ask three (or four) multiple choice questions and that they are to indicate their answers by holding up the appropriate card(s). I display the questions one at a time on the overhead or LCD projector, giving the audience time to respond to each question. I will also ask a couple of people to explain their choices. For example, in a session on time management, I might use the following questions and answers:

- My main motivation for attending this session is . . .
  a. it looked more interesting than the other sessions.
  b. to learn how to manage my time better.

    c. because my boss made me.

    d. I have no idea why I'm here.

■ As a time manager, I would describe myself as . . .

    a. organized.

    b. needing a little help.

    c. overwhelmed.

    d. hopeless.

■ My desk or work area can be described as . . .

    a. neat and tidy.

    b. organized chaos.

    c. friendly clutter.

    d. a disaster area.

■ My approach to time management is to . . .

    a. make a "to do" list every day.

    b. make a list for the week.

    c. keep a list in my head.

    d. "wing it."

People really enjoy this activity. Again, it takes little time yet gets people immediately involved in the content of the session. Notice that the questions have an element of fun to them yet also have a serious content-related component. This activity also appeals to those people who are tactile because they have an opportunity to touch and pick up the cards to show. From the speaker's point of view, the responses reveal some interesting information which the speaker can refer to throughout the session.

Paper-Tearing Exercise

To introduce the point that people are poor listeners, I explain that I am going to "test" their ability to listen and follow instructions. I explain that I am going to do the activity with them. My instructions go something like this:

- Pick up a sheet of paper and put down your pens and pencils. You will not need them for this exercise.
- Now close your eyes and keep them closed for the entire activity. Be sure to listen very carefully to my instructions.
- Fold your paper in half. Tear off the upper right-hand corner.
- Fold your paper again and tear off the lower left-hand corner.
- Fold your paper in half once more and tear off the lower right-hand corner.
- Now you may open your eyes, open your papers, and hold them up so everyone can see.

Of course, everyone has a good laugh because everyone's design is different and rarely does anyone's look like mine. I ask for one or two volunteers to explain why nobody's paper looks like mine. The response I generally get is that I gave poor instructions. I ask them how we could have ensured a better outcome. Eventually, an audience member or I make the point that two-way communication would have brought about better results. I emphasize that the responsibility for clear communication lies with both the sender and the receiver of information.

Test

At the beginning of her program on business etiquette, Marjorie Brody has audience members complete an etiquette quiz. This technique not only raises the interest level but also establishes the purpose of the speech or presentation. It sets the stage for what the speaker will be talking about. This is particularly effective for a topic such as etiquette. Quite often, participants resent being sent to a program on manners. After all, they already know how to eat and what to do. According to Brody, the smugness quickly disappears when participants are faced with questions such as the following two most frequently missed questions on the Brody quiz. (The quiz appears in the *Prentice-Hall Complete Business Etiquette Handbook* by Barbara Pachter and Marjorie Brody.)

1. True or false? In a modest restaurant, you can use your fingers to eat french fries? (Answer: False. Use your fork to cut french fries into bite-sized pieces.)
2. Who goes through the revolving door first?   a. Host b. Visitor   (Answer: a. The host goes through the revolving door first, because he knows where to go.)

The quiz creates awareness that audience members may not be as savvy as they thought they were, and that recognition motivates people to "buy" what the speaker is "selling." In other words, they're ready and willing to learn.

This type of quiz or self-evaluation can be handled two ways. One approach is to have people complete it and score it individually. Another is to ask participants to work on it with a seat partner. Working in pairs is less threatening, and it serves to generate interest and enthusiasm as the pairs discuss and debate their answers.

GET THEM ACTIVE EVEN BEFORE THE START

Bob Pike takes this immediate involvement technique one step further by getting people involved even before they start. He believes in rewarding people who come on time, particularly if the start of the program must be delayed. Pike engages participants in a "find-a-word" activity.

Collective Oral Responses

Some speakers keep their audiences involved by using a type of oral "fill-in-the-blanks." Repeatedly throughout the session, the speaker cues the audience to call out in unison the ending of a sentence that repeats the speaker's theme or key point.

A similar approach is a technique used by NSA member Willie Jolley. From the beginning, Jolley engages and energizes the audience by having its members repeat the following three-line mantra:

I feel good
I'm awake
I'm ready to learn

These techniques are similar to the coach rallying the team in the locker room before the big game. Just as the coach reinforces the team spirit, the speaker creates immediate audience bonding by giving its members a common experience. The speaker will then continue to build on and reinforce that bond throughout his or her speech or presentation.

AUDIENCE INTERACTION

Sometimes you may want your audience members to interact directly with each other. It helps them get acquainted and comfortable with each other and puts them in an active learning mode. Once again, the following activities can be used with any size group and any time frame, depending on what you want to accomplish. I have used them successfully in one and one-half hour concurrent sessions during a professional conference and in all-day seminars.

Card Sort

This activity (also from *101 Ways to Make Training Active*) is very effective in helping people learn information that has multiple sections or parts but that can be easily "chunked"; that is, broken into segments. For example, in a session on team building, I might want to introduce participants to the four stages of team development: forming, storming, norming, performing. I would create a deck of cards that consists of four "header" cards indicating the four stages and four or five descriptors for each stage, putting each descriptor on a separate card. I would create teams of four to six people and give each team a set of shuffled cards. I then instruct the teams to sort the cards, putting the descriptors under the appropriate headings. This is a great way to get people interacting while introducing them to the particular content information. This can work with any size group. I used this activity for a concurrent session at a conference in which I had six hundred people. They formed subgroups on their own when requested and spread out throughout the room finding space on the floor, if necessary, to spread out their cards.

I Don't Agree

This activity is a great way to stimulate discussion among participants and to help them gain a deeper understanding of the issue you are addressing. You start by selecting an issue or making a statement that has more than one side or perspective. For example, in a session on conflict management, you might write the following statement on a flip chart or put it on a transparency: "Conflict is healthy for an organization and should be encouraged." You then divide the audience into two sections: one group is asked to take the position supporting the statement; the other group will disagree. Depending on the size of the group, you might ask each side to form smaller subgroups or clusters to work together to come up with arguments in support of or against the statement as assigned. After an adequate time (but not too long), reconvene the entire group and ask for a spokesperson from either side to begin the debate. After a participant has had an opportunity to present one argument supporting his or her position, a member from the other side offers a different perspective. The discussion continues back and forth until all arguments have been presented or your prescribed time has elapsed. You might record the points on a flip chart or transparency and then use the information collected as a segue to the points you want to make.

Role Models

This activity is an interesting way to lead into a topic and, at the same time, to find out participants' perceptions of the subject. It is also a great way to generate interest in the topic. Put participants into subgroups of five or six and give each group a sheet of newsprint and markers. Ask each group to identify three people they would label or identify as representative of the subject under discussion. For example, in my session on leadership, I ask them to come up with a list of three people they would label "a leader." To introduce the concept of assertive versus aggressive, I ask participants to list three people they consider assertive. In both cases, they may use people who are living or dead, real or fictional. After they have identified the three well-known figures, ask them to make a list of the characteristics the three have in common that qualify them as examples or role models for the subject under discussion. They are to post their lists of people and characteristics on newsprint and post on the wall. The speaker then asks the groups to explain why they chose those particular people and characteristics.

GROUPING TECHNIQUES

In seminars and workshops, many activities require us to break a large group into subgroups. To avoid the boring and overused grouping method of having participants count off by however many groups you want to create, try other creative methods. For example, Mikki Williams puts M&M's® in the center of the table and asks participants to pick an M&M®. Mikki then asks participants to sit with those who have the same color of candy. I sometimes make or buy small jigsaw puzzles and give each person a puzzle piece. To form subgroups, the participants have to find those who have pieces to the same puzzle.

Another way to move people quickly and efficiently into different group configurations throughout the day is to create grouping cards. Each person receives a 3 x 5 card on which is a colored dot, a number, and a colorful sticker. The numbers, dots, and stickers are placed on the cards so that they will form random groups of varying sizes, depending on the purpose of the activity and required subgroup size. For example, if I have 12 people in a workshop or seminar, I will want at different times to create four groups of three (red, blue, green, yellow dots), three groups of four (e.g., zoo animal stickers: lions, giraffes, zebras), or two groups of six (numbers 1 and 2). When I am ready to put people into subgroups, I will tell them, for example, that for this activity, we will be grouping by zoo animals and I tell them what part of the room each "animal" group will occupy. If I have a particularly large group (e.g., 100), I will also post signs indicating group meeting locations to make the process more efficient and to reduce confusion.

Some speakers put colored dots or different shapes on handouts. Another idea is to use different candies, such as Hershey's® Kisses®, peppermints, butterscotch rounds, etc. You might also use different colored pens: red, blue, green, black, and so on. The possibilities are endless!

Finding Famous Fictional Friends and Families

One of my favorite ways of grouping people and having them discuss an issue related to the topic is called "Finding Famous Fictional Friends and Families." First, you create groups of four or five fictional characters in the same "family," such as Robin Hood, Maid Marian, Friar Tuck, Little John, Sheriff of Nottingham; Tin Man, Cowardly Lion, Dorothy, Scarecrow, Toto; Peter Pan, Captain Hook, Wendy, Tinkerbell, Crocodile; Hawkeye, Hot Lips, Trapper John, Radar, Klinger. Put the names of each character on a separate index card, shuffle the cards, and give each participant a card. Next, ask the participants to find the other members of their "family." When grouping is complete, ask the groups to discuss a particular topic or to come up with a list related to your topic. For example, in a customer service program, I might ask the groups to share with each other the best or the worst experience they ever had as a customer. In a program on managing change, subgroups are asked to come up with a list of the changes they are experiencing in their organizations and the industry.

Interactive Handout

Another way of involving your audience that is both effective and efficient is the interactive handout. There are several variations of this technique. One approach is to create a "fill-in-the-blanks" handout in which key words are left out (see Figure 7.1), a term is printed with space given for the definition to be written (see Figure 7.2), or a general topic is written with lines underneath indicating a series of points to be filled

Figure 7.1

Fill-in-the-Blanks

Guidelines for Delivering Super Service

1. Tell people what you _(can)_ do, not what you _(can't)_ .

2. Whenever possible, give people _(choices)_ .

3. Communicate in _(the other person's)_ style, not in yours.

Figure 7.2

Provide Definition

Approaches to Conflict
- Accommodation _____
- Avoidance _____
- Competition _____
- Collaboration _____
- Compromise _____

in (see Figure 7.3). Another approach is to list only major headings and subheadings, leaving plenty of space for note taking (see Figure 7.4). The advantage of the interactive hand-out is that the audience is directly involved and engaged throughout the process, which, in turn, enhances the connection between the speaker and the audience. Bob Pike uses this technique very effectively.

Figure 7.3

Provide Points

Characteristics of Effective Leaders

1. _____

2. _____

3. _____

4. _____

5. _____

6. _____

7. _____

Figure 7.4

Headings and Subheadings

Symptoms of Conflict
- Low morale
- Unproductive meetings
- Absenteeism
- Decreased productivity
- Accidents

Causes of Conflict
- Style differences
- Value differences
- Perception differences

To make your handout even more interesting, be sure to use graphics and to include an icon on each page that illustrates a theme, your client's business or industry, or even your client's logo. For example, I might use an icon representing a "beaker" if I am addressing a chemical company, a dollar sign for a financial services company, a medical symbol for healthcare, different geometric shapes for diversity, or a businessman and businesswoman holding briefcases for a management development session.

The Power of Two

Asking two people to work together is another easy and efficient method of audience interaction. We noted earlier the use of pairs in "Active Knowledge Sharing." You can use this technique of asking people to work together for a variety of purposes. You might ask them to come up with a list of something, such as characteristics of an effective leader or customer expectations. You might also ask people individually to write down their personal goals or a personal action plan at the end of a session and then share them with their partners.

Creating Synergy

This activity is used to promote cooperative learning and to reinforce the importance and benefits of the message that two heads are better than one. List topic-related questions on the flip chart, transparency, chalkboard, or participant workbooks. Then ask participants individually to answer the questions. After all participants have completed their answers, arrange them in pairs and ask them to share their answers with each other. The next step is for pairs to create a new answer to each question, improving on each person's response. When all pairs have written new answers, one member from each pair will report to the entire group.

REGAINING CONTROL

Speakers are often reluctant to have participants interacting with each other, especially in large groups, because they are afraid of losing control and of not being able to get the group's attention again. This is not a problem if you do a little planning and communicating up front. First, be very clear and specific when telling them what you want them to do; second, give them a time frame; and finally, tell them what signal you are going to use to let them know when time is up. There are many ways of regaining the audience's attention, both auditory and visual. Bob Pike, a master of the interactive presentation, uses the multiple clapping method. For example, when he wants to call the group back to order, he will ask the audience to clap once if they can hear his voice and he claps once. Then he asks them to clap twice if they can hear his voice, and he claps twice. Finally, he asks them to clap three times if they can hear him, and he claps three times. By that time, people have quieted down and refocused their attention on the speaker.

Another master of audience interaction is Mel Silberman, who uses a train whistle to reconvene the group. I use a variety of sounds, including a cow bell, siren, police whistle, sleigh bells, horn, and kazoo to get the audience's attention. They never know what sound to expect and love the surprise.

Some speakers use visual signals, such as turning the lights on and off or holding up a sign or object. I sometimes use what looks like a fly swatter in the shape of a hand in a neon color.

Audience involvement and participation can focus on each individual member of the audience, not just on the group as a whole. For example, to drive home the point that change is uncomfortable and requires us to think about changing our behaviors, try this activity. Ask audience members to get comfortable, sit back, relax, and fold their arms. Then ask them to unfold their arms and put them down to their sides and shake them out. Next ask them to fold their arms again but this time fold them the opposite way. You will notice people trying awkwardly to fold their arms. Ask them how it felt: Some will say "uncomfortable"; others will say "awkward." If no one mentions it, you should ask if they had to think about it. Then drive home your point by telling them that change requires us to abandon old behaviors and embrace new ones. And just as they were uncomfortable folding their arms differently, they will be uncomfortable with the new behaviors at first.

Audience participation can involve the entire audience, an individual, or several people who become representatives of the audience as a whole. Participation involving an individual or a representative sampling requires more direct interaction with the presenter. We will address this strategy in more detail in Chapter 8.

Interacting with Your Audience

Interacting with your audience is somewhat different from involving the audience. As we saw in Chapter 7, audience involvement incorporates techniques such as working with a seat partner or in a small group. However, these techniques do not lend themselves to direct speaker interaction with the audience. Although there is audience involvement, the speaker is simply orchestrating or choreographing the involvement or interaction of audience members with each other. This chapter, however, focuses on direct interaction between the speaker and the audience—individually or collectively.

SPEAKER–AUDIENCE INTERACTION

Talk Show Host Techniques

One of the most effective techniques used by speakers to interact with the audience can be found by watching television talk show hosts. Notice that they get up close and very personal with the audience. First, they physically move into the audience. They step down from the stage and make their remarks while standing in the aisle a few rows into the audience. This has the advantage of making the audience members feel that the speaker is one of them. It breaks down the invisible barrier created by the space or distance between the stage or platform and the first row of seats. A disadvantage, of course, is that the people in the first few rows may feel left out because the speaker has his or her back toward them. If you choose to use this technique, be sure not to spend too much time in that position. Also, when you move back to the front of the room, back out of the audience rather than turning your back on the audience and walking forward. Some speakers ensure that their audience remains close to them by actually extending the stage into the audience. They purposely place props and other materials a few rows back so that they have to walk into the audience.

To loosen up the audience and to create a light, low-risk environment, I will walk into the audience with a toy microphone that lights up and has swirling glitter when you shake it. I ask individual audience members to speak into my "magic microphone." It helps them focus on the silly prop rather than themselves.

Other speakers will actually sit in the audience and even deliver a part of the presentation from their seats. The benefit here is that when they get up and move to the platform, the audience, in essence, goes with them. The result is immediate rapport.

Get to Know Your Audience

Talk to participants before the session either by telephone or by arriving early to meet and greet people as they come in. Engage them in conversation and find out a little about them. Be sure to get their names so you can refer to them specifically in your session. Of course, ask their permission to use their names and/or stories and comments. Tell a story or anecdote and substitute a participant's name as the key character. In a corporation, you may want to use the name of the CEO or the department manager. Once again, be sure to get permission and make sure that the story doesn't embarrass anyone.

Ask Questions

One way of connecting with the audience is to pose a "safe" question and ask for volunteers to share their answers. For example, Glenna Salsbury asks, "What's the best book you've read recently?" Hands shoot quickly in the air as audience members are eager to share their own "must read" choices. This technique helps Glenna connect with her audience and also gives her some insight into their interests.

Questions, of course, are a must in a longer session such as a seminar, workshop, or conference breakout session. Questioning is an art and one that can be mastered easily by remembering to use two key words: *what* and *how*. We have all learned somewhere along the way that we should concentrate on asking open-ended questions rather than close-ended questions to stimulate discussion. As a refresher, close-ended questions can be answered with a simple "yes" or "no." For example, "Would you like to elaborate on that?" The danger here is that the receiver could easily answer, "No," and the discussion is over. On the other hand, an open-ended question is designed to get the receiver to open up, share additional information, or expand on his or her points. Consider the following questions:

- ▪ "What has been your experience in this area?"
- ▪ "What led you to that conclusion?"
- ▪ "How could you apply that to your situation?"

Any one of these is far more effective in getting the other person to elaborate on his or her points and to create a real interaction between the speaker and audience member. Try to avoid starting a question with "why." A "why" question puts people on the defensive. For example, if you ask someone, "Why do you believe that?" the receiver's reaction is to justify his or her position. Setting up this type of defensive posturing does not promote positive interaction.

AUDIENCE RESPONSE SYSTEMS

An effective method of interacting with the audience, regardless of size, is to ask questions and to use various audience response systems to capture their responses. The simplest approach is to ask for a show of hands. Glenna Salsbury poses three simple questions and asks audience members to respond by simply raising their hands. As a variation, you might also choose to ask a question and call on two or three individual audience members to respond.

Low-Tech Methods

Another interesting and graphic way of getting everyone to respond is to use Responder Cards. To answer multiple choice questions, each audience member is given a set of four different colored cards, each marked with the letter *A, B, C,* or *D*, as I used with the "Instant Assessment" activity described in Chapter 7. For true–false questions, participants receive two cards, each of a different color and marked with the letter *T* or *F.* The speaker asks questions and then asks participants to indicate their answers by holding up the appropriate cards.

If you don't want to deal with the headache of preparing sets of cards (I once had to make 600 four-card sets for a conference presentation), a less labor-intensive approach is the stand-up/sit-down method of responding. For example, in a session on managing conflict, I prepared the following statements about conflict with which participants were asked either to agree or to disagree:

- Conflict is inevitable.
- Conflict can produce either creative or dysfunctional results.
- Conflict increases during times of change.
- Conflict is the same as disagreement.

As I show each statement, I ask people to stand up if they agree with the statement and to stay seated if they disagree. I will call on one or two people to explain briefly why they responded the way they did.

A variation of the physical movement approach is to present three or four multiple choice questions. Instead of holding up cards, I ask people to respond with the following movements:

- **Choice A**—Raise one arm in the air
- **Choice B**—Raise two arms in the air
- **Choice C**—Stay seated; no arms raised
- **Choice D**—Stand up

Once again, I ask a couple of people to explain their choices.

High-Tech Approach

A more sophisticated and high-tech response system is the electronic keypad. With this system, each audience member is given a keypad that is connected to a computer. When the speaker shows the question or item on the screen, each person indicates his or her answer by pushing the correct button on the keypad. The responses are collected in the computer, and the data are instantly projected so that the entire audience can see the results.

Making It Meaningful

With all these methods, it is important to take the time to process each answer briefly before going on to the next item. Simply call on two or three people to explain their thoughts or rationale in choosing their particular responses. These response methods serve several purposes. They give the speaker an opportunity to learn more about the audience and either their knowledge of or their attitude toward the subject. The activity itself helps to introduce the audience to the topic and serves as an icebreaker.

Sometimes, you may want the audience to indicate a choice or preference among three or more options. A purely subjective but fun way to get them to respond is with an informal "Applause Meter," which "registers" their level of enthusiasm, shown by thunderous clapping or whooping and hollering. You would determine the results by using your own sense of the most popular choice and simply announce the winner or create a fake "Applause Meter" and move the meter to suggest the level of response. For example, let's take the two wrapped boxes mentioned in Chapter 5. To get an overall impression of the group's preference, I would hold the boxes up, one at a time, and ask the audience to indicate by clapping which one they would choose.

Sharing Examples

Audience members love to learn from each other, and many are eager to share their own experiences. An effective technique is to ask if anyone in the audience has a personal example to share that might further illustrate your point or that you can use to work through an example or model. The benefit of this technique is that people in the audience can identify with "one of their own." The real stories add credibility to your points and validate their own beliefs and behaviors. Keep in mind that this can be risky. For one thing, the participant's response might not be what you're looking for, and then you're faced with the dilemma of having to move on to someone else and possibly embarrassing your eager volunteer or struggling to make the example fit with your point. Another danger is that when participants are given an opportunity to share a story or example, they sometimes go on and on, providing unnecessarily detailed explanations. If you choose to solicit examples and stories from the audience, be aware that this participation will take longer than you originally anticipated, so be ready to make adjustments in your presentation. You might be able to exercise some degree of control by telling the group that you are only going to take a specific number of examples and that you would like them to limit their remarks to a specific number of minutes. The more you can prescribe specific guidelines, the better your position of control. Better still, ask people ahead of time to share their experience and be very specific in the guidelines and state how long you want them to respond.

Throughout your session, speech, or presentation, remember and refer to comments audience members have made earlier in the session. This, of course, is easier to do in a breakout session or seminar.

SHARING THE SPOTLIGHT

You can bond quickly with your audience by sharing the spotlight. When you establish a relationship with one member of the audience, you automatically create a relationship with the entire audience. Through this one person, you create a sense of intimacy with everyone that allows you to enter their hearts and souls with your words.

The most important thing to remember when inviting audience members to share the stage is to create a risk-free, comfortable climate right from the beginning. After all, being on stage puts the person in a highly vulnerable position. First and foremost, don't do anything that will embarrass your audience volunteer and never pressure or coerce someone into participating. Start with someone you have chosen and coached before the presentation. If there is something the person needs to read or prepare, give it to him or her well before the session starts so he or she can become comfortable with it. Once audience members see their cohorts enjoying themselves on stage, they will begin to relax. By the time you ask for volunteers, people in the audience will be clamoring to participate.

To illustrate the power of coaching and encouragement, I ask for a volunteer to come up and explain that when I say, "Go," I want him or her to make as many hash marks as possible on a flip-chart page during a 45-second period. I also instruct the audience to remain silent during the timed activity. At the end of 45 seconds, I call time and ask for another volunteer to come up to coach the first person to try to beat his or her record. I give the "coach" a hat and let the coach spend a couple of minutes with the first volunteer to discuss strategy. Before I begin the next timed session, I ask the audience to whoop and holler and do whatever they feel will encourage and help the volunteer to do better. I also instruct the coach to use his or her coaching skills to help the volunteer improve over the first time. I begin the second 45-second timing, during which the audience is calling out supportive messages and general words of encouragement. They really get into the cheerleading mode. At the same time, the "coach" offers suggestions to help the person do better. Without fail, there is always improvement the second time around.

USING ROLE PLAY

It's a good idea to seek out volunteers before the session and explain to them what you want them to do. Even then, be sure to start with a fairly safe interaction or activity that will help put audience members at ease and relieve any tension they may be experiencing out of fear of being called on. In training sessions, in particular, the often-dreaded role play is an important part of the learning process. When people hear the term *role play,* they immediately picture being called to the front of the room and asked to "perform" the skills they have learned in the session. There are various nonthreatening ways to get people involved in a role play, even on stage.

Scripted Role Play

You might start with a demonstration role play. A demonstration role play is fully scripted, so that participants just have to read the dialogue of their assigned parts. In selecting your actors, be sure to ask them early in the session, preferably before you begin or at break. The important thing is to give them enough time to practice reading their lines and to get comfortable with their roles. It would be helpful for you to give them a little coaching as to how you want them to act.

At "show time," you will explain to the audience that you are going to conduct a demonstration role play, and they are to watch carefully and to take notes on what the characters do well and on what areas need improvement. After the "actors" have finished the scenario, they sit down and I conduct a discussion with the group, noting both the good points and the bad points. For example, I use the following scripted role play in a sales management training session for a pharmaceutical company:

> *Scenario:* Roberta (or Robert), a sales training manager, has accompanied a new sales representative, Sam (or Samantha), on his (or her) sales calls. The two have called on four physicians so far. It's near the end of the day, and the sales training manager suggests that they stop at a coffee shop for coffee and a debriefing session before they call it a day.
>
> *Instructions:* As the two volunteers read the following role play, please observe carefully and take note of (1)

what the sales training manager does well in providing feedback and (2) in what ways he or she could improve.

R: It's been a pretty exhausting afternoon, hasn't it?

S: Boy, I'll say! Some of these docs can be really difficult to deal with.

R: Well, that's what I want to talk to you about. I thought this would be a good opportunity to give you some feedback on what I observed and also give you some suggestions to help your calls go more smoothly. After all, both your goal and mine is to help you make more sales. Right?

S: Absolutely. Okay, let me have it.

R: Let me start by saying that I think one of your biggest assets is that you are very warm and friendly. That really helps in establishing rapport with the customer. You have a great personality, and you do a great job of connecting with the docs.

S: That's good to know. I've been told that I have the gift of gab and can sell anything to anybody.

R: You certainly have the talent. All we need to do now is to fine-tune those skills. One of the things you have going for you is that you seem to know the products well. It's obvious that you're well versed on the features and benefits of each product. You do a good job of getting the main points across in a very limited amount of time. Do you agree?

S: Absolutely. I'm really confident that I know the products.

R: Since product knowledge is not a problem, we need to take a look at what is getting in the way of a really successful sales call. The biggest thing I notice is that in your eagerness and enthusiasm, you aren't taking enough time to plan your sales call. As a result, you come across as disorganized and appear to be flying by the seat of your pants. That's one thing. The second problem I see is that you seem to be a little too eager to close the sale based on what the doctor says he or she needs instead of taking the time to analyze the situation. Do you know what I mean?

S: I'm not sure I do.

R: For one thing, you don't ask enough open-ended questions to uncover what the doctor's needs really are. Because you know the products so well, you seem to focus on just telling the doctor about the products. I also think that you need to do a better job of really listening to what the doctor is telling you. I don't think you're picking up on the cues. What I would recommend for your next set of calls is to do a better job of pre-planning, concentrate on asking probing questions, and really listen to the doctor's response, and that includes body language as well. Other than those few things, I think you're doing a good job. So, do you think you can work on those things I just mentioned?

S: Well . . . okay.

R: Good. I'm sure you'll see a big difference the next time out.

You can use the scripted role play at the beginning of a session to get the audience thinking about the topic and to set the stage for your learning points. You can also use it at the end of a particular section as a way to review and reinforce the learning. These scripted role plays can be as long or as short as you like and can therefore be used in a training session, breakout session, or even keynote.

What Should I Do?

Another type of nonthreatening role play involves asking a volunteer to join you on stage with the volunteer assuming one role and you assuming the other. Although this role play is not scripted, you will, of course, explain what you want your fellow actor to do or say. As you conduct the role play, you stop the action at various intervals and turn to the audience and say, "What should I do?" Then you call on an audience member to coach you by telling you what you should do or say next. You then resume action and apply what your coach told you to do. Each time you stop, ask a different person for advice. For example, you might want to demonstrate the correct approach for dealing with a chronically tardy employee. The scenario would play out something like this:

Speaker:	I want to talk with you about a performance issue. I've noted that in the past two weeks, you have been late six times, ranging from 10 to 20 minutes each time.
Volunteer:	I know I've been a few minutes late, but it's not a big deal. I manage to get all my work done.

At this point, the speaker stops the interaction, turns to the audience and says, "What should I do?" Let's assume an audience member suggests that the speaker tell the "employee" that he or she must get there on time every day. The action resumes.

Speaker:	I know you get your work done, but that's not the point. I expect you and everyone else to get here on time every day.
Volunteer:	I really try, but things come up. Yesterday I missed my bus, Tuesday my alarm didn't go off, and last week, my babysitter was late; I couldn't leave until she got there. Besides, Ann is late lots of times, and you don't say anything to her.

Again, the action stops, and the speaker turns to the audience for advice once more. The role play can continue as long as the speaker wants; however, I recommend only three or four stop-action opportunities for audience input. Otherwise, the audience could get bored. Be sure to tie it to your learning points by emphasizing how the audience's suggestions reflected what they learned about dealing with a difficult employee.

Spontaneous Role Play

With this technique, the presenter or trainer once again plays a role. Before you conduct a spontaneous role play, be sure to model or demonstrate what you want the audience member to do. For example, in my session on "The Art of Influencing," I introduce the audience to a model they can use when giving feedback to a colleague, family member, or friend. I first take them through the model using something personal from my own experience to illustrate the steps. I then ask for someone to volunteer to share his or her own situation and a person to whom he or she would like to give feedback. When the volunteer joins me on stage, I ask questions to help set the scene and coach him or her through the model. This technique has been extremely successful because the rest of the audience members can relate to a real scenario and can see immediately how they can apply it to their own situation.

Demonstration Role Play

Although time consuming, this method gives participants a way to practice specific skills. For example, in a session on managing conflict, the trainer creates several different conflict case scenarios and assigns a scenario to each group of three or four people. The groups are given 15 to 20 minutes to discuss and analyze their cases and prepare role plays to demonstrate how they would use collaboration or cooperation to resolve a conflict. Using our conflict example, one group receives the following scenario:

Conflict Case
You are a hard-working, dedicated employee with a lot of self-motivation. You thrive in an environment where your manager tells you what needs to be done and then lets you do it. Not only do you not need close supervision, you find it stifling and demotivating. Unfortunately, you work for a manager who likes to take a real hands-on approach. He or she likes to know what's going on at all times. Your manager frequently stands over you while you're working on a project and sometimes asks what is preventing you from finishing. The truth is that his or her hovering not only annoys you but also makes you nervous. As a result, your productivity slows down and you are more prone to make mistakes.

When the group presents the role play, it goes something like this:

Employee:	I think I understand that you like to keep on top of things and like to be kept informed of my progress on this project. When you keep coming to my desk and looking over my shoulder, I become distracted and find it difficult to focus on my work. I would like to suggest that we find a way that you can be kept up to date on the project and I can have the time I need to work on the project uninterrupted.
Manager:	I'm sorry if I make you nervous or distract you, but that's my style. I like to know what's going on at all times. I need to have all the answers when my boss asks me how the project is going.
Employee:	I can imagine that it would be uncomfortable and embarrassing if you weren't able to answer Ms. Smythe's questions. How about this? You and I could meet for a few minutes at the end of each day so I can give you a complete update. If it would help, I could also give you a written progress report at the beginning of every week. That way you will have all the information you need and I will be able to concentrate on completing the project on time and on target. How does that sound to you?

Rotating Trio Role Play

This technique gives people another opportunity to practice the skills taught in a training session. It, too, is time consuming, requiring approximately an hour to complete. Participants form groups of three, and the trainer asks each group to

develop three real-life scenarios related to the topic. Another
option is for the trainer to create the three role plays and for
all trios to use the same three scenarios. In either case, each
scenario will be the basis for a role play, and each person will
assume a different role for each of the three rounds. For
example, I use the following three role plays in a program on
coaching skills for sales managers in a pharmaceutical setting:

Trio Role Play #1
You are a new sales representative and are about to have
a meeting with the sales training manager. You have not
been satisfied with the outcome of some of your sales
calls. In particular, you have a physician/client who gives
you the rush every time you call on her. She has a very
busy practice and is obviously a no-nonsense, get-to-the
point person. In fact, she even says to you, "Okay, you
have two minutes to tell me what you have to tell me.
I'm very busy, and I have a waiting room full of patients
who need to see me." Her only concern is to get you in
and out of the office quickly, and, in fact, she shows her
impatience by looking at her watch frequently while you
are talking. You want the sales training manager to tell
you what you can do to get more time with this physician and others like her.

Trio Role Play #2
You are a new sales representative and are about to have
a meeting with the sales training manager. You have not
been satisfied with the outcome of some of your sales
calls. In particular, you have a physician/client who
keeps promising to use (Specific Product) but doesn't. You
have called on him several times and have detailed him
thoroughly on the product. Every time you call on him,
he says he will use it with his patients, but he still
doesn't prescribe it. He seems to be knowledgeable about
the product and is very positive when you talk with him.
Nevertheless, you continue to experience delay after
delay. He doesn't raise any objections about the product,

so you have no idea why he has not even used the many
samples of (Specific Product) you have left with him to
try with his patients. You want the sales training manager to tell you what you can do to get this physician to
prescribe (Specific Product) for his patients.

Trio Role Play #3

You are a new sales representative and are about to have
a meeting with the sales training manager. You have not
been satisfied with the outcome of some of your sales
calls. In particular, you have a physician/client who
objects to prescribing (Specific Product) because it is too
expensive. You have done a good job of detailing the
product and have stressed the many benefits of this drug.
This physician, however, focuses only on the price and
not on the value of the product. After all, he can prescribe a less-expensive drug manufactured by your competitor. You want the sales training manager to tell you
what you can do to overcome not only this physician's
resistance but also the resistance of others who may raise
similar objections to this and other company products.

The following describes the *sales manager's role* for each
role play:

You are the sales manager and are about to have a
coaching meeting with one of the new sales representatives. The sales rep wants some direction from you on
how to handle a particularly difficult physician/client.
Your job is to help the sales rep by coaching him or her
on how to deal with this particular type of problem person. Your approach should focus on helping the sales
rep problem-solve for himself or herself by following the
problem-solving model of diagnosis, alternative actions,
and consequences. Use open-ended questions to encourage the rep to think about the problem, think about
things he or she may not have considered previously,
and generate for himself or herself various approaches to
the problem and their resulting outcomes.

Finally, the *observer* is instructed as follows:

As the observer, your job is to observe and give feedback
to the sales training manager on his or her skill in
demonstrating effective coaching techniques with the
new sales representative. The sales training manager
should follow the problem-solving model of diagnosis,
alternative actions, and consequences. When presenting
your feedback, focus on the sales training manager's
skill in asking open-ended questions to help the sales
rep think about the problem, to think about things he
or she may not have considered previously, and to generate for himself/herself various approaches to the problem and their resulting outcomes.

RECRUITING VOLUNTEERS

You can ask for audience volunteers well into your presentation after they have had an opportunity to size you up and
you have earned their confidence and trust. When using a
volunteer, explain what you are going to ask a volunteer to
do on stage. People are wary of a speaker who says, "I'd like
someone in the audience to join me on stage. Do I have any
volunteers?" The audience is suspicious, and rightly so. For all
they know, you are going to have them do something that
could result in making them feel foolish.

Reward Your Stars

Be sure to reward those who volunteer by first acknowledging
their willingness to take a risk and thanking them for being
such good sports. Lead the applause to show appreciation and
support for the volunteers and then give them a gift.

Some speakers are known for their immediate rewards
and reinforcement techniques, such as throwing candy or
other small prizes to those who participate or respond to a

question. It's amazing how effective this can be in encouraging people to speak up and get involved.

GETTING IMMEDIATE FEEDBACK

An important part of audience interaction is getting feedback from audience members about their level of satisfaction with the session as well as their suggestions for improvement. Many speakers distribute a 3 × 5 card or a small sheet of paper and ask participants to respond to two questions:

- What did you like best about the session?
- What needs to be changed or done differently?

The speaker gets immediate and meaningful feedback, and audience members get to both offer their suggestions as well as receive kudos, and they also experience a sense of satisfaction when they see the speaker collect the feedback on the spot.

Handling Questions

The question-and-answer period can be a speaker's boon or bane, his or her shining moment or worst nightmare. A poor Q & A period can ruin a good presentation. Many speakers don't recognize the value of the Q & A session. Rather than dread the question-and-answer period, speakers should view it as an opportunity to further clarify, convince, and connect with their audience. It can serve as a forum to make an even bigger impression on the audience because it allows you to showcase your ability and expertise. It allows you to reinforce your points and to communicate your earnest desire to meet audience members' needs and to address issues of vital concern to them.

The Q & A session can also be a mine field if the speaker is not prepared or loses control of the situation. If it is handled improperly, the speaker can lose credibility and create a variety of negative perceptions.

REASONS PEOPLE ASK QUESTIONS

Some speakers believe that a formal question-and-answer session is a waste of time. They argue that if they have delivered a good speech, presentation, or seminar, the structured session is unnecessary. So before we address some of the dos and don'ts of fielding questions from the audience, let's look at the reasons people want the opportunity to ask questions. Understanding their motivation will help you better prepare for both the expected and the unexpected.

They Want Information or Clarification

No matter how good the presentation or how clear you were in delivering your message, the people in your audience will not all process and understand the information in the same way or at the same time. Some will want and need additional information to help them understand your points more clearly or to satisfy their desire for more detail. They may want further assurance that you know what you're talking about. Something you said during your presentation may have ignited a spark of curiosity or provoked an interest to find out how they might learn more about a topic on their own. In the latter case, they will ask questions about other resources and will expect you to point them in the right direction. Even if you have provided a bibliography or recommended reading list, some will want you to recommend your favorites or to identify sources for specific interests and pursuits.

They Want to Impress Others

Every group has one or more people who like to ask questions as an opportunity to get noticed either by peers or by someone at a higher level whom they want to impress. Being in the spotlight may satisfy some people's ego needs. For others, it affords them the chance to demonstrate qualities such as assertiveness and risk taking or to showcase their knowledge of the subject as a means to career advancement.

They're Out to Get You

For various reasons, many of which we will explore in Chapter 10, some audience members or participants won't like you or what you have to say. They view the Q & A period as an opportunity to make you look bad or to see you squirm in the hot seat purely for their own amusement. They may see this as a chance to "get even" or to undermine your credibility.

They Want to Help the Speaker

At the other end of the scale, you will have audience members who really like you and want to help you look good. If they agree with your position on a particular topic, they will want to help you increase your persuasive impact even more.

They Don't Want to Go Back to Work

Some people in the audience or training session may ask questions as a way to avoid returning to work, particularly if the session is over near the end of the day. They may reason that the more questions they ask and the more time they can take up, the less time there will be to get anything accomplished back on the job and so they might as well go home.

GENERAL GUIDELINES

Set the Ground Rules in the Beginning

Before you launch into your presentation, tell the audience members that you will be taking questions and let them know when. Audience members can ask questions during the presentation, at the end, or before breaks. In a training session, I encourage people to ask questions as they think of them. Sometimes, however, I need to limit the number of questions or the time spent addressing them in order to stay on schedule. The important thing is to communicate clearly when you will and won't take questions. Often speakers don't like to be interrupted because it breaks their train of thought and the flow of their presentation, and their irritation shows.

If you want to wait until the end, say so. You might suggest that if questions pop into their minds during your session, they should write it down so they don't forget it. Tell them how much time you will allot to the question-and-answer session. If your time is limited, you might assure them that you will be available for individual one-on-one questions after the session is over. Then, of course, make sure you stay around and don't rush off to catch a plane to your next speaking engagement. Also, mention that in the interest of time and to ensure that everyone has an opportunity to be heard, you will limit the questions to one per person. Finally, be very clear about areas you consider to be off limits. Be polite but firm in telling the audience what you are and are not willing to address.

GETTING STARTED

Priming the Pump

Have you ever experienced the following scenario? You have just finished your presentation. You delivered your message flawlessly, and the audience response indicated that you were an overwhelming success. As your meeting planner requested, you left plenty of time for questions. So you introduce the Q & A session by asking, "Are there any questions?" Your question is met with stony silence, and you say to yourself, "What do I do now? I have 15 minutes left?" Often, speakers who find themselves in this situation try awkwardly to fill the extra time by adding more content and pieces of information. This is not a professional approach and becomes anticlimatic. Other speakers will simply say something like, "Well, I guess I covered everything. So thank you for coming," and walk off the stage. Both these approaches leave the speaker feeling very awkward and the audience members sensing that something is missing—that there are loose ends. Both the speaker and the audience leave the experience dissatisfied and unfulfilled. To jump start a reluctant audience, you might try the following techniques.

Communicate Your Desire to Answer Questions

The way in which you introduce the question-and-answer period is critical. You need to communicate a genuine desire to answer questions by saying something like, "I'll be happy to answer your questions now." Further support this statement with positive nonverbal posture and gestures. For example, move out from behind the lectern. Men might even consider taking off their jackets. Move closer to the audience. Some people find it very effective actually to leave the platform and move into the audience. If you recall the 1996 presidential campaign, you might remember how effective Elizabeth Dole, candidate Bob Dole's wife, was when she left the stage and delivered her speech to the Republican delegates on the convention floor. She exuded warmth, charm, and sincerity, in part because it's her natural style, but also it was the result of eliminating the distance and invisible barrier between her and her audience.

Planted Questions

Before your presentation, you could ask one or two people to pose a question you have already prepared. It is important that you not only write out what you want them to say but also that you give them ample time to become comfortable with the question so that it sounds natural and not like a planted question. You may also give them a signal so they know when to ask the question. For example, when you make a certain gesture, such as taking off your glasses or scratching your nose, the person should then raise his or her hand and pose the question. Once things get started, other people in the audience will be prompted to pose questions.

One of the benefits of planted questions is that they prevent the awkwardness of waiting and hoping someone will speak up. It increases your comfort level and boosts your confidence because you know what the question is and have a well-prepared answer. On the negative side, however, the "plant" may be obvious, and the audience will resent being manipulated. Another potential blunder might be that the "plant" will either forget his or her cue or decide to phrase the question quite differently from what you had planned.

Index Cards

If you are afraid that you might not get any questions and are not comfortable with the approaches already mentioned, you can distribute 3 x 5 cards to audience members and tell them to jot down any questions that come to mind as you are delivering your remarks. Further explain that you will then collect the cards at the end of the session and answer as many as time permits. This technique is both efficient and nonthreatening. Often, people who are reluctant to speak up in front of a large group will feel more comfortable writing the question. This is particularly effective when the topic is a sensitive one. For example, in a session on business etiquette, managers may be too embarrassed to ask questions about dining dos and don'ts for which they think they should already know the answers. In corporate audiences made up of people from all levels in an organization, individual employees are sometimes afraid of asking a question for fear of retaliation or looking bad in front of their peers or supervisors. The index card technique provides anonymity and gives participants an opportunity to think through their questions and to be clearer and more concise.

Group-Generated Questions

Depending on the amount of time you have and the size of
the audience, you can ask participants to take a few minutes
to gather informally in small groups or pairs to generate one
or two questions per group. You can then have a spokesperson for each group stand and ask the question, or you can
use the index card technique described earlier. Breaking into
small groups to develop questions will give everyone an
opportunity to be heard. This technique also creates less
exposure for you and gives you a greater degree of control.
You can control how much time will be spent allowing the
groups to generate questions, and you also control how the
questions will be presented. For example, if you are afraid
that certain outspoken people will dominate the small-group
discussions, you can be creative in designating discussion
leader and/or spokesperson. You might say that the
spokesperson for each group will be the one whose birthday
is closest to today or who traveled the farthest or who had
the largest number of graduates in his or her high school
class. Bob Pike uses a finger-pointing technique that's always
a lot of fun. He asks people to point their fingers in the air
and instructs them to point their finger at someone in their
group when he gives the signal. Those who have the most
fingers pointing at them are now the designated spokespeo-
ple. As a variation, the designated spokesperson in each group
can then choose someone else.

Ask and Answer Your Own Question

As a last resort, if no one asks a question, you might try pos-
ing a question yourself and answering it. You can simply say
something like, "I'm sometimes asked . . . " and then provide
the additional information.

PLANNING AND PREPARING

Anticipate and Prepare

The best advice for shining in a Q & A session is to prepare, prepare, prepare! You should plan as carefully for the question-and-answer session as you do for your presentation. Spend time brainstorming by yourself or with someone else to come up with questions you might be asked—no matter how remotely possible or bizarre. Write down the potential questions and also write your answers. Rehearse your answers just like the rest of your presentation. The idea here is to avoid surprises. Be sure to have facts, figures, and other appropriate documentation with you just in case you need to substantiate or back up your points. Ideally, you should have a summary of this information on a visual that you can easily retrieve and show to the audience. Invariably, someone will challenge you just to prove a point or may simply want to know where to go for more information. Be sure your information meets the following criteria:

- Your information should be current. That means that you must have the most up-to-date figures and recent developments. The Internet is a valuable resource for keeping abreast of changes and trends in an industry or specific organization.
- Accuracy is also important. Double-check the information, particularly when dealing with statistics in research studies. You may encounter conflicting numbers, so be ready to cite your source and provide the necessary backup data.
- Make it relevant. The data you use needs to be relevant not only to the topic but also to the group. If you cannot find information directly related to the group's specific business, use facts and figures from a related industry.

■ Your source(s) must be credible. Use only credible sources for your information. Credible means that the information can be validated. For example, you can be reasonably confident that information culled from a recognized and respected source such as *The New York Times* or *The Wall Street Journal* is reliable. On the other hand, you will be on very shaky ground if you quote articles appearing in a supermarket tabloid.

TAKE CARE OF LOGISTICS

Whenever possible, for large audiences, request that audience microphones be made available. And either request that those who have questions come to the stationary floor microphone or have two or three assistants armed with traveling microphones that they can quickly and easily take to the audience participant.

ADDRESSING THE QUESTION

Eye Contact and Other Nonverbals

Good eye contact is just as important during the question-and-answer period as during the presentation. When answering a question, first look at the person who asked the question to acknowledge and verify the question. Then look at the entire group. Keep in mind that your answer is a mini presentation itself.

As hard as it may be, particularly if you're under fire, do your best to smile. Not only will it help you convey warmth and sincerity, a smile can serve to disarm your attacker.

As mentioned earlier, step out from behind the lectern and assume an open, nondefensive posture; that is, don't fold your arms. Your posture should convey confidence but not stiffness.

Repeat the Question

Speakers should get in the habit of repeating the question, even if the audience member is using a microphone. By repeating the question, you accomplish three things:

- You are making sure that the rest of the audience has heard the question.
- You are making sure that you have heard the question correctly.
- You are buying yourself a little time to better organize your thoughts before answering.

Use Active Listening Skills

Have you ever been in a situation in which the speaker's answer to a question was totally off the mark? Most probably the "disconnect" was a result of the speaker not taking the time to clarify and confirm what he or she thought the participant actually asked. Sometimes, the person asking the question is not as articulate as we would like and may have a difficult time stating the question concisely and succinctly. To ensure that the question received is the same as the one intended, paraphrase the question by saying, "If I heard you correctly, your question is . . . Is that right?" If the question is long, ask if you may reword it, then restate it concisely and check to see that you indeed captured the essence of the question. Don't, however, paraphrase by using any of these phrases:

- "What you mean is . . . "
- "What you're saying is . . . "
- "What you're trying to say is . . . "

These phrases are insulting and condescending. The subtle message is: "You bunny brain! You're obviously not articulate, so let me help you out."

Keep Your Answers Short

This is not an opportunity to deliver another speech. If you launch into a lengthy explanation or discourse, your audience members will hesitate to ask another question. After all, they don't want to become permanently attached to their seats.

Here are two other reasons to keep your answer short.

1. The audience may perceive your long explanation as an indication of insecurity or defensiveness.
2. A long, laborious answer eats into time and cuts down on the number of people who can ask questions.

Also, don't engage in a lengthy discussion with any one person. Again, although you are addressing a question asked by one person, your answer should be delivered to the entire audience.

Deliver your answer in a conversational tone, free of jargon and multisyllable words. Use examples that audience members can relate to or identify with in order to illustrate your points. I often use parenting examples, but I always ask, "How many of you are parents?" before I make the analogy. If there are few parents in the audience, I will suggest that people think about the parenting example from their experience as children.

Choose Your Words Carefully

Choose your words carefully and think about the impact they may have on individual audience members. Avoid using words such as *obviously*. This implies that the person asking the question should already know the answer. Along the same line, phrases such as "You have to understand . . . " come across as ordering and directing. "You should . . . " is seen as preaching or moralizing.

Avoid qualifiers such as "I think," "I believe," or "I feel." These phrases diminish your effectiveness, make you sound tentative, and convey a lack of confidence. Besides, since it's your answer, your thoughts, feelings, or opinions are implicit in the statement. Try to use strong, powerful words to convey your meaning. As we discussed in Chapter 6, the more graphic the word, the more impact it has. For example, if you are responding to a question about the financial picture of your organization, you could simply answer, "Business is good and we should expect to see a record-breaking year." But think about how much more impact and meaning your answer would have if you said, "Business is booming. The demand for our services has skyrocketed. Since we repositioned ourselves in the marketplace, profits have soared."

Use Neurolinguistic Programming

Try to use some NLP (neurolinguistic programming) techniques to identify and then choose words to match the questioner's preferred sensory mode. For example, if a questioner says, "What do you *see* as the biggest challenge facing the speaking industry?" you might respond by saying, "I *view* the biggest hurdle to be technology." Notice that both the question and the answer are visual. On the other hand, an auditory questioner would more likely say, "I've *heard* that it's almost impossible to make a living as a full-time speaker. Do you agree?" and your matching response would be, "That statement *sounds* a bit strong." Finally, a question such as "Do you feel motivational speakers are in less demand?" indicates that the person asking the question is probably kinesthetic. To match his or her sensory mode, you would say, "Sometimes it's hard to get a handle on these trends." NLP takes a lot of study and practice; however, you can train yourself to listen carefully to the other person's word choice and then

deliberately choose an appropriate sensory word for your
response. It just takes practice.

Formula for Success

Your answers to audience-generated questions should be
delivered with the same clarity and coherence as your main
presentation. You certainly don't want to come across as a
bungling, inarticulate idiot. The ability to think on your feet
requires both skill and artistry. A sure-fire way to deliver your
answers with polish and professionalism is to use the three-
part formula used for "Table Topics" by Toastmasters International. Think of your answer or conclusion first, but don't
begin by stating it. Instead, use the following approach:

- Begin by repeating or paraphrasing the question.
- Next, give supporting points or a brief explanation.
- Finally, conclude by making your main point.

To see how this works, consider the following scenario:
You have just delivered a presentation on employee motivation and an audience member asks you this question: "What
if you've already tried all the suggestions you just mentioned,
but nothing seems to work with some employees?" Here is
your answer using the Table Topics formula:

- **Paraphrase**
  "It certainly can be frustrating when you've tried a number of motivational techniques or strategies and nothing
  seems to work."

- **Support or explanation**
  "Occasionally, you may encounter someone who, despite
  your best efforts, just won't budge. As we're told by motivation experts and theorists, motivation is something that
  comes from within. Your job as a manager is to create a

positive environment in which people are motivated. Just like everything else in life, motivation is a two-way street."

■ Conclusion

"Sometimes, you have to accept the fact that some people, for whatever reason, can't or won't allow themselves to be motivated. In that case, concentrate on the other 99 percent who will."

GUIDING PRINCIPLES

Respect the Audience

Never belittle or embarrass an audience member. That means that sometimes you have to exercise a little patience, particularly when someone asks a question that you have already addressed in your presentation. Absolutely never say, "As I already mentioned during my presentation . . . " Instead, answer the question by carefully rewording your point so that you are not repeating the remark exactly as you said it earlier.

Responding to Individual Concerns

Sometimes, an audience member will ask a question that is extremely narrowly focused and pertains only to the person asking it. If that happens, give a brief response and then suggest that the two of you talk about it after the session. Use this same strategy with those who ask questions unrelated to the topic. Always indicate your openness and willingness to talk further, one-on-one. Above all else, you want to project compassion and concern.

Limiting Questions

Believe it or not, there are some people who just love to hear themselves talk! These folks are bent on asking question after question. Once again, be clear at the beginning of your Q & A session that you want to give everyone a chance to ask questions. For that reason, you will be limiting each person to one question. After everyone who wants to be heard has done so, you can allow people to ask additional questions.

Cover All Parts of the Audience

Speakers sometimes have a tendency to look only to their right or to their left and, as a result, to entertain questions from only one side of the audience. Although this is unintentional, people on the side being ignored will become anxious and annoyed. Similarly, some speakers will acknowledge questioners who are in the front because it's easy to both see and hear them. Make a concerted effort to take questions from all parts of the audience.

Don't Bluff

People may ask questions that you can't answer. Be honest. Don't be afraid to say, "I don't know." However, don't leave it at that. Offer to check further and to get back to them by phone or mail or tell them where they might get the additional information themselves. Be sure to ask for the person's business card and write down what information he or she needs.

Maintain Control

Never let someone take the platform away from you. Some will try by launching their own mini speeches; others through personal attacks. Remember that it's *your* stage. You're in control. Be polite but firm when suggesting that "we" need to move on.

Handle Challenges with Grace and Professionalism

Accept the fact that you are not always going to be correct. If someone points out an error and you believe that that person is correct, thank the individual for pointing it out to you. Whatever you do, don't get defensive. An individual may challenge you by offering a different opinion or point of view. When that happens, acknowledge the difference of opinion and thank the person for offering a different point of view. Don't, however, get into an argument or a debate. People automatically ask questions that start with "why." Quite naturally, you feel challenged and have a tendency to react defensively. To avoid delivering a defensive-sounding response, first reframe the "why" into a "how" or "what" question when you restate it. For example, if someone poses the following question, "Why did you . . . ?," you would reframe it by saying, "If I understand you correctly, you're asking me *how* I . . . " Or, "As I understand it, you want to know *what* I . . . " When responding to these challenging questions, begin with, "In my experience . . . " or present facts or quote experts as appropriate.

AVOIDING PITFALLS

Things Not to Say

In an effort to be supportive and encouraging, speakers will often respond to a questioner by saying, "That's a good question." The danger here is that you may come across as patronizing or insincere. Also, others who do not receive the same feedback or reinforcement may feel their questions weren't as good. Instead, comment by saying, "That's an interesting question," or, "That's an intriguing question." Similarly, a response such as "I'm glad you asked that question" may be understood by others to mean that you aren't glad they asked a question. Be careful not to use "I'm frequently asked that question." This response could convey that this person's question is not particularly special. This response could also cause the audience to pause and wonder, "If this is such a common question, why didn't the speaker address it in his (or her) presentation?"

Another no-no is "Does that answer your question?" What happens if the participant responds that you didn't answer the question? Worse still, the questioner may not have had his or her question answered but doesn't want to embarrass you or himself/herself and just lets it go. By asking if you answered the question, you give up some control and you suggest a lack of confidence in your answer. A better response would be "What other questions do you have?" or "Would you like me to go into more detail?" This is a much more gracious and face-saving approach for both the speaker and the questioner. It also gives the questioner an opportunity to clarify his or her question or to probe a little further, if necessary, so that he or she is satisfied.

Sending Mixed Messages

Speakers sometimes say they want questions, but their body language says otherwise. For example, if the speaker assumes a defensive posture, such as folding his or her arms, that's a sign that he or she is really not open to questions. Another real turn off (and an incredibly rude gesture) is to roll one's eyes. Also, I've seen speakers in the process of packing up and getting ready to leave. The message here is "Your questions are getting in my way. I'm outta here." Speakers must demonstrate congruence between their words and their actions. How you handle yourself at the end of your session will leave a lasting impression on the entire audience.

FIELDING CURVE BALLS

Personal Questions

Audience members may ask questions that are in poor taste. They may enjoy getting under your skin or they may just want to get to know you better as a person. Although politicians and other public figures are the most common targets of direct, personal questions, no speaker is exempt. The best way to handle an inappropriate personal question is to answer it as tactfully as possible and move on.

Personal Attacks

Personal attacks may be triggered by something you say that strikes a nerve in an audience member, or the attacks could come from a professional heckler who just enjoys the challenge of putting you on the spot and making you squirm. The best strategy to use with the heckler is just to ignore the person. If his or her behavior becomes really disruptive, quietly ask someone in authority to remove the individual from the audience. Hecklers are often found in audiences when participants have been socializing a little too much before the presentation, such as at a dinner meeting with a cocktail hour preceding it. Invariably, an individual will have one too many and will then make a fool of himself or herself by trying to bring you down.

Far less annoying but still offering a real challenge is the person who begins attacking you because he or she disagrees with something you said. For example, when I was conducting an all-day workshop for a group of managers, I was talking about the importance of managers communicating clearly their standards of performance and expectations to their employees. I also emphasize the need to include guidelines or parameters as part of those expectations. I decided to use a personal parenting example to illustrate my point. I had learned through earlier questioning that 95 percent of the audience members were parents. I related an incident involving my stepson many years earlier, when he was 14. I created the appropriate backdrop for the situation by explaining that 14-year-olds go through the "black period," during which everything they wear is black. So when my stepson wanted to redecorate his room, I thought it would be prudent to tell him that he could decorate his room any way he wanted except for two things: he could not paint his walls black, and he could not put up posters of nude women. The audience laughed as always when I tell that story. Before I could go on to draw a parallel between parents setting parameters and managers doing the same, I was interrupted by a man yelling at me from the back of the room: "How could you do such a thing? That was your son's room, and you have no right telling him what he can and cannot do with his own space!" As he continued his ranting, I interrupted by saying, "I can certainly understand your point of view, however, we're not here to debate parenting philosophy. I was making a point that, just as parents have the right to set standards and expectations for their children, managers have the right to set standards and expectations for their employees. And in both cases, one person's standards may be quite different from another's. The important thing is that you clearly communicate them and hold people accountable."

KEEP YOUR COOL

When faced with the unexpected, the most important thing to remember is to maintain your composure. You must remain calm and in control. Several techniques will help you in these situations.

- **Lower your pitch.** When we get nervous or upset, the pitch tends to get higher, particularly with women.
- **Breathe deeply.** Shallow breathing is a sign of nervousness and will affect the quality of your voice.
- **Control your speed.** Many people have a tendency to speak faster when they are under stress, so concentrate on maintaining a moderate rate when responding.
- **Control your volume.** Although you want to project your voice, don't yell. Maintain a reasonable volume level, loud enough to make sure you're heard but not so loud that you sound angry or out of control.
- **Attend to nonverbals.** Avoid nervous gestures such as fiddling with clothes, jewelry, paper clips, pointer, etc. Those are a dead giveaway that you are losing control. Also, be careful not to appear in a counter-attack mode; that means if you are gesturing, keep your palms open and don't point.

ENDING THE QUESTION-AND-ANSWER PERIOD

Ending the question-and-answer period should be done with the same care and planning as ending your main presentation. Don't keep asking, "Are there any more questions? Are you sure no one has anything else he or she wants to ask?" When it appears that the questioning period is winding down or if you are at the end of your time, simply summarize the additional points that have been raised and how they relate to the key points. Then thank the audience for attending. Enough said!

10 Dealing with Problem Situations

No matter how well you have planned and prepared for your speech, presentation, or seminar, you can be certain that more often than not, you will be faced with the unexpected. Too often, what started out as a terrific session turns into your worst nightmare.

Some human behavior, attitudes, or reactions are predictable. It's our job as professional speakers, trainers, and seminar leaders to anticipate these behaviors, to prevent them if we can, and, if we can't, to deal with them effectively.

UNDERSTANDING DYSFUNCTIONAL BEHAVIOR

In order to prevent dysfunctional behavior, we need first to understand it.

Causes of Dysfunctional Behavior

People Don't Want to Be There

People often resent attending a session. Perhaps they feel they are being punished, or they may feel overwhelmed by their workload and don't believe they can afford to take time away from the job. For example, I was asked to conduct a session on performance appraisal for first-line supervisors in a manufacturing setting. During my assessment meeting with the vice president of operations, I sensed that there might be some resistance to the training. So I discussed with the vice president the importance of explaining to the supervisors why the company was investing time and money in this program and how they could benefit from attending. The vice president confirmed that he would communicate that message. The morning of the session, I met briefly with the vice president, who assured me that he had prepared the participants as I had suggested. Breathing a sigh of relief, I walked into the room only to be confronted by 19 frowning men seated in a horseshoe configuration with their arms folded. Although the situation did not look good, I was confident that I could bring them around. I started with an appropriate icebreaker and opening activities. The supervisors absolutely refused to participate. After several failed attempts to break through the stone wall of resistance, I stopped and said, "Guys, it's clear to me that something's going on here, and I think we need to talk about it. Let me ask you a question. Why do you think the company is offering this session?" With that, the flood gates opened, and I was bombarded with comments such as "Beats the [expletive] out of me" and "I guess we must be doing a pretty [expletive] job and now we're being punished." I spent the next 45 minutes just talking with the group members and helping them see how this session could help them do their jobs better. Clearly, the vice president had not done his job.

In another situation, a colleague and I were conducting a three-day "Train-the-Trainer" program. The participants did not want to be there and made no attempt to hide it. They openly stated that they didn't see any reason to be there— they already knew how to make presentations, and since they worked in a sales organization, they were being taken out of the field during their busiest season. As an added complication, they had not been told that training was now going to be part of their jobs. The dysfunctional behavior ranged from outright rudeness, such as multiple side conversations and getting up and walking around the room, to hostile remarks and nonverbal disrespectful behaviors, such as one person putting his feet up on the table. The next morning, the group was taken to task by the representative from the corporate office, who chastised them for their behavior. Although their behavior improved somewhat, they were still difficult. Later that evening, the participant who was the most difficult talked with me informally and mentioned that they had been "called on the carpet" that morning and were told they had offended my colleague and me. He justified his and others' behavior and told me, "Frankly, I don't care if we offended you. Our company is paying you a lot of money to do this program, so we can treat you any way we want to." He went on to tell me that he was missing an important social event that would have afforded him the opportunity to network with his clients.

People Don't Know Why They're There

Believe it or not, some people walk into a session and have no idea why they were asked to attend. Sometimes, they don't even know what the topic is. I had been engaged to do a two-hour session on communication for line employees at the plant site of a packaging company. As I frequently do, I asked the participants why they were there and what they hoped to learn in the session. I was surprised to learn that they thought they were attending a safety training session. Talk about the need for communication training!

Personal Issues

Session participants are human beings, and human beings have personal lives and problems that sometimes get in the way of learning new things. They may be preoccupied with a personal problem, or they may simply not feel well. I have had a group of people who were all in the midst of relocating. They were understandably preoccupied with the challenges and stresses of selling houses, buying new ones, and making arrangements to move. They were up and down, in and out during the entire session.

Sometimes the personal issues are not apparent. In one situation, I was conducting an all-day workshop for bank branch managers. To make a point about the importance of reward and reinforcement as motivating factors in employee performance, I have the group participate in an experiential activity called the "M&M® Game," found in *Session Builders 200*, published by Training Resource Corporation.* I form teams of five people and assign the following roles: one person is the manager, one person is an observer, and three people assume the roles of employees. While the "employees" for each group settle in different locations, I ask the "managers" and "observers" to join me in the hall. I give each "manager" three sets of four paper-and-pencil activities (one set for each "employee") and a cup of M&M's® I instruct the "managers" to mentally identify their "employees" as Employee A, Employee B, and Employee C. I then tell them that they are to go back into the room and ask the "employees" to complete the paper-and-pencil tasks. Throughout the activity, the "managers" will reward the "employees" as follows:

- The "manager" will give M&M's® to Employee A periodically (and for no reason) as Employee A is working on his or her task. The "manager," however, is not to say anything to this "employee."
- The "manager" will give verbal praise and encouragement to Employee B but will give one or two M&M's® only when the "employee" finishes each task.
- Employee C will receive no praise, no words of encouragement, and no M&M's® until he or she is finished with all four tasks. The "manager" can then give Employee C four M&M's®.

---

*Reprinted with permission: Session Builders 200, © 1986, Training Resource Corporation, Harrisburg, PA, (800) 222-9909.

The "managers" along with the "observers" return to their groups and carry out their instructions. The reaction among the "employees" is always quite interesting. Even though they know it's just a "game," those playing the roles of employees really react to the way they are being rewarded or ignored by the "managers." After the activity is completed, I call the entire group together to discuss the activity, and particularly the reactions of those who played "employees." On this particular occasion, I started the discussion by asking those who played the managers to share their reactions to the activity. One "manager" (we'll call him John) was quite eager to share his experience. I wasn't surprised that John was first to volunteer. He was very outgoing, displayed a great sense of humor, and had been very participative throughout the session. He was a man of about 55, with a husky build and sporting a full beard. I was surprised, however, at John's reaction. He started by saying, "I'm very upset with this activity." I then asked him to elaborate. He continued with "I . . . I . . . I . . . " and then he began to cry and was unable to continue. I apologized to him and the rest of the group and reminded them that this was an activity, a game, designed to illustrate a point.

About this time, a sound from my left caught my attention. I turned to see another participant, Anna, sobbing uncontrollably. At this point, I stopped the planned debriefing and spent the next 45 minutes helping the participants deal with the emotions this activity brought out. The discussion was very helpful and everyone seemed okay when we broke for lunch—except for Anna. At the break, I went to Anna and put my arm around her, told her I was sorry the activity had upset her, and asked her what was wrong. She told me that she reported directly to the CEO of the bank, who was a real tyrant. The only feedback he gave his employees was negative feedback when they did something wrong. Otherwise, he ignored them. She went on to say that in this activity, she identified with Employee C, the one who was given no praise and no rewards. The activity brought forth the raw emotions lurking just beneath the surface and for so long suppressed. The message here is that many of our audience members or participants bring a lot of emotional baggage with them to our sessions. And we have no way of anticipating how something we might do or say might trigger an intense emotional reaction.

Attitude toward the Boss or Organization

If a participant has negative feelings about the organization or his or her manager, he or she will bring that negativity into the session. The resentment is transferred to the speaker. Since the boss or the organization hired you, you are guilty by association and automatically viewed as "one of them."

Sessions dealing with change present a particular problem. For many, the session only serves to magnify the change or changes they are experiencing, and in many cases, the participants are not happy about these changes. In a program on "Managing Change and Stress," at the beginning of the session, I asked participants to share the most difficult or troublesome change they were currently experiencing. One man was quite emotional when he related that his difficult change was moving his office from the suburbs to the city. As the day progressed, we learned that he had been with the company 30 years and enjoyed six weeks vacation and a very comfortable salary. In our discussion about values, he was quite clear that money, material possessions, and his vacation time were very important to him. At one point in the program, I made a point that in dealing with change, we all have choices, and those choices are based on many things, including our values, personality type, family situation, and so on. As I finished my statement about having a choice, this man started yelling at me: "You don't understand! I don't have a choice in moving my office! I'm sick of you high-priced consultants coming in here and telling us what we should do. You have no idea what you're talking about. . . . " He continued his tirade, and I sat down and allowed him to run out of steam. After he was finished, I told him that I could see his point and that I was sorry this change was causing him such distress. Very likely his feeling of powerlessness and the resulting anger and frustration had been smoldering for some time. The discussion triggered an intense emotional response that was really directed toward the company. Although he may have seen me as a representative of the "enemy," I was in no position of power, and therefore, was a safe target on which to unleash his pent-up hostility.

Attitude toward the Topic

Not all audience members or participants will be happy with the topic, particularly if their attendance has been mandated. This is particularly true when you are presenting controversial topics such as diversity or sexual harassment. Some participants have been quite candid about their perception that the topic is "being shoved down our throats." In a session for a group of bank managers on sexual harassment, one man expressed his disapproval of the entire subject by saying, "If women don't like the way they're treated, let them go work elsewhere."

Literacy Problems

If people have difficulty reading, they will be resistant to attending a session that may require them to do anything that involves reading, such as using case studies, written exercises, and assessment instruments. I once had a participant who did not show up for the first session of a four-part supervisory skills program and called me at home on a Friday evening to explain why. He told me that he was 55 and had been with the company for 30 years. He went on to say that he had not come to class because he was afraid. He couldn't read and he didn't want "the guys," his buddies, to find out. The guys told him that I was really good and the class was interesting. But the guys also told him that I had them working in groups doing cases studies and other activities that required reading. He told me that he really wanted to come, but he didn't want anyone to know about his reading problem. I assured him that I would communicate orally the instructions and anything else he needed to know so that no one would have any idea that he couldn't read.

In another supervisory training session, I had distributed and asked the participants to complete a self-assessment instrument. After I gave the instructions and the participants began filling out the assessment, I noticed one woman in the back who seemed to be struggling with the assignment. After observing her for several minutes, I concluded that she couldn't read. So I went back, sat down next to her, and quietly read the questions. In both cases, I accommodated their special needs, and they were able to participate fully in the session.

Language Problems

For those who are not fluent in the language in which the session is being delivered, the experience can be frustrating and unpleasant. Because of their frustration and difficulty in understanding what the speaker is saying, they may act out their frustration by being difficult and uncooperative, either intentionally or unintentionally. As our audiences become more diverse, this issue will become an even greater challenge for us as speakers.

Past Experiences

Some participants may have had unpleasant learning experiences, either in school or even as adults attending other work-sponsored programs. They may come to the session expecting it to be much of the same, and they are braced to expect the worst. This sometimes comes out at the end of a session. Depending on the group, and particularly if I sensed some resistance early on, I will ask the group during the feedback portion near the end of the session the following question: "Was this program different from what you expected?" The answer is always "yes," and when I probe further, participants tell me that they expected it to be dull and boring. Some will say that they thought I would just lecture or talk at them. They will often add that my approach was a pleasant surprise and made the experience both meaningful and enjoyable.

The Effects of Dysfunctional Behavior

Now that we have looked at the causes of dysfunctional behavior, let's take a look at the effects. Left unchecked, dysfunctional behavior can divide the group into various factions, polarizing them against you or each other. These negative behaviors also interfere with learning. No one can learn in an environment dominated by disruptive behavior. Finally, these undesirable behaviors cause emotional stress and anxiety for those who are witnessing the shenanigans.

PREVENTION STRATEGIES

Now that we know the causes and effects of dysfunctional behavior, let's take a look at what we can do to prevent behaviors that get in the way of a super presentation.

Planning

We have already addressed the importance of finding out as much as you can about your audience through the use of questionnaires and surveys, participant interviews, and discussions with the meeting planner and/or participants' managers. It's also a good idea to send something to the audience members ahead of time. It might be an interesting, attention-getting flyer, a short article to read, or anything that will pique the participants' interest and prepare them for the session. This is particularly important if you are conducting a seminar or workshop. With longer sessions, you might assign readings or other work to be completed ahead of time.

Preparation

When designing your training session, writing your speech, or preparing your presentation, consider the various learning styles and perceptual modalities we discussed in Chapter 2. Be sure to use interactive techniques and don't be afraid to be creative, even outrageous. Also use a variety of methods and media to appeal to various styles.

CONTROLLING YOUR ENVIRONMENT

In many cases, you won't be able to do anything about the seating arrangements or configurations, particularly with large audiences. At general sessions during conventions, theater-style seating is the norm; for dinner or luncheon speeches, the audience will very likely be seated at round tables seating 8 to 10. With smaller groups, however, you are more likely to have control on how you want the seats arranged. This is particularly true with seminars and workshops. Even in situations in which you cannot move the chairs, keep in mind that you can, however, move the people. You can ask people to get up and move to different areas of the room and stand during a brief, small group discusssion. You can also ask people to reposition themselves in their chairs in order to form small discussion groups.

Seating Configurations

Part of the planning process is deciding how much partici-pant interaction and speaker or instructor control you want. Then you choose the seating arrangement conducive to creat-ing that desired outcome.

NSA member Paul Radde, an expert in audience-centered seating, suggests following six basic principles for effective room setup:

■ Set to the long side of the room.
■ Semicircle the seating for visibility and absolutely no straight rows.
■ No middle aisle. Flare aisles to the 1:30 and 10:30 clock positions.
■ Face each chair directly toward the presentation.
■ Cut single-row access lanes in large sections.
■ Set the last row to the back wall.

Consider the following seating arrangements and what they are designed to accomplish:

Theater or classroom
■ Formal atmosphere
■ Low group involvement
■ High degree of control by presenter
■ Primarily one-way communication
■ Participant movement limited

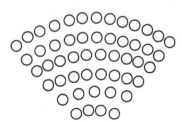

Horseshoe

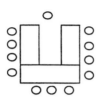

- Semiformal atmosphere
- Moderate group involvement
- Presenter in control
- Some two-way communication
- Allows for some participant movement

Square or round tables

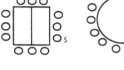

- Informal, relaxed atmosphere
- High participant involvement and interaction
- Presenter becomes part of the group
- Facilitates problem solving and promotes open discussion

Cluster

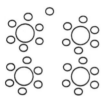

- Semiformal atmosphere
- High participant involvement
- Presenter serves as facilitator
- Emphasis on small-group work
- Freedom of movement for both presenter and participants

Conference

- Formal atmosphere
- Moderate participant involvement
- Presenter clearly in control

Semicircle or circle

- Very informal
- High participant involvement
- Allows for changing configurations
- Conducive to a variety of activities and interactions

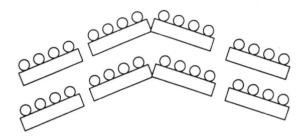

Chevron

- ■ Somewhat formal
- ■ Low to moderate participant involvement
- ■ Allows for some interaction
- ■ High degree of control by speaker
- ■ Limited participant movement

Creature Comforts

You may have little or no control over things such as lighting and temperature control. But you can use activities or plan interactions that will take participants' minds off their discomfort. Get them up and moving. Have them work in small groups or pairs. Once they are engaged in an activity, they won't have time to focus on the less-than-ideal physical environment.

Create an Inviting Atmosphere

For full-day or half-day sessions, make sure you request (or bring yourself) the accoutrements that help create a professional environment. These include tent cards, paper and pencils, water, quality participant materials, and maybe even dishes with wrapped candies. This communicates an important message to the participants: This session is important. A professional touch will help set the tone and make it more difficult for people to act up. For sessions of three hours or more, make sure there are refreshments available during breaks. Not only is this reflective of a professional touch, but also it shows consideration for the participants. During an all-day session for a trade association, the meeting planner and I learned a valuable lesson about the importance of meeting basic needs. The meeting planner had arranged for coffee and tea to be available when participants arrived for the work-shop. The participants, however, noted on their evaluation sheets the conspicuous absence of donuts, muffins, or bagels; their disappointment impacted the overall rating of the ses-sion. Keep in mind that many people in today's audiences forego the traditional coffee and tea in favor of soft drinks, juices, and bottled water. Health-conscious and calorie-con-scious participants also prefer fresh fruit to pastries and other foods loaded with fat and sugar.

The majority of people attending meetings, seminars, and conferences are baby boomers. They are sophisticated and demanding. They want the comforts of home plus the tech-nology of the office. They are also very health conscious. Responding to their special needs, hotels and conference sites offer healthy meals and plenty of recreational facilities. Not only are these amenities important for the physical well-being of meeting participants, but also they provide network-ing opportunities and stress release.

DEALING WITH DYSFUNCTIONAL BEHAVIOR

Regardless of Your preventive measures, you may find your-self faced with a particularly difficult audience. Sometimes audiences or groups as a whole behave as a single entity. The key to dealing with these situations is to be able to size up your audience and quickly adapt your style accordingly.

The Relaxed Group

A relaxed group is characterized by its warmth and friendli-ness. It is clear from the beginning that members have a positive attitude toward you and the program. They are lively and are eager to participate. This group is a speaker's dream. You should, therefore, mirror their warmth and friendliness. Smile and use lots of eye contact. Use this opportunity to try new activities and materials. Be animated and use lots of gestures and movements.

The Serious Group

These people take themselves and their work very seriously. They prefer a matter-of-fact, no-nonsense approach. To connect with this group, you should be very organized and use facts, figures, and research studies to support your points. Be sure to stick to the agenda and start and end on time. Be warm and friendly with the appropriate amount of professional restraint. Avoid using gimmicks or being "cutesy." Your props and other visuals should reflect the serious nature of the group.

The Indifferent Group

People who create the indifferent group may or may not want to be there. Their behavior at times may reflect a somewhat short attention span. The key to reaching them is to be entertaining and dynamic, using a highly interactive approach. Use lots of eye contact, movement, and gestures. Also use humor, cartoons, anecdotes, and flashy visuals. Be sure to organize and present your content in a concise, easy-to-follow format.

The Hostile Group

The hostile group presents quite a challenge. These people clearly don't want to be there, and they make it known from the very beginning. Although the reasons are not always apparent, they may resent you and/or the topic. Because they are looking for opportunities to embarrass you, they constantly challenge you or try to take control. We will discuss the specifics of dealing with hostile situations later in the chapter. However, in general, try to remain calm and controlled. Gradually express your natural warmth and friendliness. To avoid giving them ammunition for personal attacks, limit your use of personal stories and anecdotes and try to control your animation. Always use objective material to support your points. Be well armed with facts and figures from credible sources. To support your position, use favorable quotations from authorities, especially those from people who are normally associated with the opposite point of view.

Speakers must sometimes accept the fact that some people are just rude and obnoxious. If that's the case, there's nothing you can do to change the behavior except handle yourself with grace, dignity, and professionalism. As the saying goes, "Never let them see you sweat."

DEALING WITH PROBLEM PARTICIPANTS

More often than not, the group as a whole is not a problem, but there may be a few difficult people in our audiences. (I recently had a group of 15, each of whom represented each of the difficult character types we're going to take a look at.) So here are some coping strategies for dealing with specific character types and their behaviors.

Talkative

The talkative participant has something to say about everything. This person always volunteers to be a group leader, to answer questions, or to offer suggestions. He or she seems to want to be the center of attention. To deal with the talkative type, you might say something like, "I appreciate your contribution, but let's hear from some other people." You might also suggest further discussion at the break or lunch by saying, "In order to stay on schedule and on track, let's discuss this further during the break or after the session."

Clueless

This person seems to have no idea of what's going on. He or she totally misunderstands the question or the topic being discussed. As a result, this person's answers or remarks don't even remotely relate to the subject under discussion. For this person, your strategy would be to say, "Something I said must have led you off track. What I was trying to say is . . . "

Rambling

The person who rambles goes on and on about nothing. He or she digresses frequently and uses examples and analogies that don't relate to the topic being discussed. This person is different from the clueless individual in that the rambler knows what's going on but prefers to follow his or her own agenda. To get this person back on track, try asking, "I don't understand. How does this relate to what we're talking about?"

In a seminar or workshop, an effective technique is to suggest that the question or issue be put in the parking lot. The parking lot is simply a sheet of flip-chart paper posted on the wall and having easy accessibility for all participants. When issues arise that are not related directly to the topic or questions are asked that you cannot answer immediately, these items are listed on the flip-chart page to be addressed later.

Belligerent

The belligerent person is openly hostile, challenging and arguing about every point. This person questions the presen-

ter's knowledge and credibility and may even accuse the presenter of being out of touch with the real world. Whatever
you do, don't engage in any verbal sparring. Say to this person, "I understand and appreciate your point of view. What
do some of the rest of you think?" By turning to the rest of
the group, you get yourself off the hook and give others an
opportunity to exert some peer pressure to change this person's behavior. You might also offer to discuss the issue further during break.

Stubborn

This individual refuses to see anyone else's point of view. This
person is particularly difficult to deal with in a team environment. Coming across as an obstructionist, by refusing to give
in on a point, he or she will thwart group decision-making or
consensus-seeking activities. You might have to take the
direct approach and say, "I appreciate your position (or point
of view), but for the sake of the activity (discussion, etc.), I'm
going to insist that we move on. I'll be happy to discuss this
with you later."

Silent

Every audience or group has one or more silent types. This
person seems attentive and alert but will not volunteer comments or answer questions. He or she may be naturally shy or
uncomfortable speaking up in a group and seems content just
to listen. You might ask yourself, "So what's wrong with
that?" The problem is that these quiet people often have
some wonderful comments and contributions to make, and if
we don't make an effort to involve them, their ideas never
surface and the group misses the opportunity to learn from
another of its members. Try prompting the reluctant or shy
participant by saying, "(Person's Name), I know you have

some experience in this area. It would be helpful if you would share your thoughts with the group." Another approach is to break the group into pairs or trios. The shy person is much more likely to participate in these smaller groups.

The Know-It-All Individual

The know-it-all individual often tries to upstage or overshadow the presenter. Often viewing himself or herself as an authority on every subject, this person assumes a superior role with both the group and the presenter. This person relishes the opportunity to flaunt his or her knowledge, often using big words, quoting facts and figures, and dropping names. Although this situation is often difficult, don't let your annoyance show. Acknowledge his or her contribution by saying, "That's one point of view. However, there are other ways of looking at it."

Class Clown

The class clown is relatively harmless unless you allow him or her to get out of control. This person makes a joke out of everything and goes out of his or her way to get attention, often at the expense of others. Don't give in to this person's attempt to control the situation. Simply say, "We all enjoy a little levity. But right now, let's get serious and concentrate on the topic at hand."

Negative

This individual complains about the organization, his or her boss, coworkers, you name it. In addition to the negative verbal remarks, he or she displays negative nonverbal behavior such as frowning or assuming a defensive posture. Often, this person is a chronic complainer who has nothing positive to contribute. Say something like, "I understand your point. What suggestions do you have to change the situation?" Or you might say, "For the sake of discussion, what might be some arguments for the opposite point of view?"

Indifferent

It's pretty clear to you and the rest of the group that this person does not want to be there. He or she makes no attempt to participate or contribute. Because he or she has been forced to attend, not only will this person show no interest but also he or she may even resort to engaging in his or her own activities separate from the group. Use a tactic similar to the one you might use with the silent type: "I know you have some experience in this area. Please tell us . . . "

Personality Clashes

In some groups, you may have people who just don't get along. They engage in verbal battle either directly or indirectly, often with remarks becoming very personal and hurtful. When a situation like this occurs, it is important to address it early on by invoking ground rules or by saying, "I suggest that we keep personalities out of the discussion. Let's get back to the topic at hand."

Side Conversations

Side conversations are a frequent and annoying occurrence. Far too often, two or more members of the group engage in their own conversation while fellow participants and/or the presenter is talking. You might need to try more than one strategy to bring them back. Sometimes, just walking over to the individuals will cause them to stop their conversation. If that doesn't work, try saying, "(Persons' names), we were just talking about . . . What are your thoughts?"

GENERAL GUIDELINES

When dealing with any of these situations, keep in mind four important goals:

1. **Stop the dysfunctional behavior.** Your first objective is to get the person or persons to stop the disruptive behavior.
2. **Keep the individual(s) engaged.** Your second objective is to prevent the person from "shutting down" and not participating at all.
3. **Keep the rest of the group involved.** Your third objective is to prevent others in the group from shutting down. Keep in mind that others will judge you by the way you handle these difficult situations.
4. **Respect the individual.** Your fourth objective, and perhaps the most important, is to respect the individual and help maintain the person's dignity. Whatever you do, don't embarrass or belittle.

Once you have addressed a behavior or responded to a hostile participant, look to another person or section of the audience. Continued eye contact will only further encourage the participant and may result in a continued debate or argument. Remember that you can never win an argument with a participant. Even if the group is annoyed with their fellow participant's behavior, if you attack that person, the others may turn against you. After all, he or she is one of them.

When participants demonstrate intense negative emotions, it's important to acknowledge those feelings and emotions with a statement like "I can tell you feel strongly about this" or "I'm sorry you feel that way." Be careful not to make judgmental statements like "You're being negative" or "You're not listening."

BE CREATIVE

Set a creative tone by using music and posters. As we discussed in Chapter 6, use themes and line the walls with posters and quotations that reflect or relate to the topic. Not only do these extra touches engage the audience, but also people recognize and appreciate the extra effort it takes to plan, prepare, and produce "a show."

LEARN FROM YOUR MISTAKES

Sometimes your problems don't surface until after the session is over, when participants have the opportunity to "get you" on the evaluation sheet. On more than one occasion, I have been completely surprised and taken aback by someone's comments. For example, I conducted a day-long session on "Influencing Others" for 25 management trainees. The group was quite diverse in terms of race, ethnicity, gender, and cultural backgrounds. The session was going quite well with lots of participation and interaction. Even at breaks, the participants were eager to discuss the topic. In particular, I spent time at breaks and at lunch talking at length with one young man whose homeland is Afghanistan. He was also quite participative during the session, and I thought I had established real rapport. I was quite astounded and disturbed when I read my end-of-session evaluation from this man. He gave me very low marks because he "was offended because you made no attempt during the day to use my name." The fact that there were others whose names I did not mention apparently didn't matter. I had insulted this person by my unintentional omission.

LEARNING TO LIVE WITH IT

I have learned to accept that in some cases of problem participants, I had no way of knowing their personal problems. In others, I cry *mea culpa* and learn from my mistakes, and in still others, I did everything in my power to prevent the situation from getting out of control. Unfortunately, the ugly truth is that people bring a lot of baggage to our sessions that we have no way of knowing about or controlling.

I once conducted a two-day "Train-the-Trainer" session for bank trainers. The entire group was difficult, but one young woman in particular was very uncooperative and resisted learning new training techniques. This young woman, in her mid-20s, remarked several times during the program that "older" people (later defined as 40-plus) didn't take her seriously and didn't respect her knowledge and experience. She also mentioned that most of her trainees were in their teens. She made very disparaging remarks about these folks as well. She gave me the lowest ratings possible on my evaluation and wrote scathing remarks that were very personal attacks. I, of course, was quite upset and talked to her manager, who had hired me. During my conversation with the manager, I discovered that this young woman has demonstrated immature behavior and poor interpersonal skills. Her manager described her as insecure and threatened by those who are older and more experienced. Apparently, these emotional hang-ups influenced her behavior in class and her unwillingness to learn a new approach.

Remember the red suit incident? Although I certainly could not have anticipated this person's reaction, the incident illustrates the impact that seemingly small, insignificant details have on certain individuals. It also had quite an impact on me. I don't think I have worn a red suit in front of an audience since!

Appendix: Resources

Giveaways

Best Impressions
> P.O. Box 802, LaSalle, IL 61301, 1-800-635-2378

Parkway Business Promotions
> 4875 White Bear Parkway, White Bear Lake, MN 55110
> 1-800-562-1735

Sales Guides, Inc.
> 4937 Otter Lake Road, St. Paul, MN 55110, 1-800-352-9899

Humor

The Humor Project
> 110 Spring St., Saratoga Springs, NY 12866,
> 1-518-587-8770

Magic

Tricks for Trainers, by Dave Arch (book)
> Creative Training Techniques Press, 7620 West 78th
> Street, Minneapolis, MN 55439, 1-800-383-9210

Hank Lee's Magic Factory
> Mail Order Division, P.O. Box 789, Medford, MA 02155
> 1-781-391-8749 or 1-800-874-7400

Abbot's Magic
> 124 St. Joseph St., Colon, MI 49040, 1-616-432-3235

Magic, Inc.
> 5082 N. Lincoln Ave., Chicago, IL 60625, 1-773-334-2855
> or 1-888-550-1022

Music

American Society of Composers, Authors, and Publishers (ASCAP)
  One Lincoln Plaza, New York, NY 10023, 1-800-627-9805
Broadcast Music Inc. (BMI)
  320 W. 57th St., New York, NY 10019, 1-800-669-4264
Creative Training Techniques Press
  7620 West 78th Street, Minneapolis, MN 55439,
  1-800-383-9210

Props, Toys, and Training Tools

Creative Learning Tools
  P.O. Box 37, Wausau, WI 54402, 1-715-842-2467
Creative Training Techniques Press
  7620 West 78th Street, Minneapolis, MN 55439,
  1-800-383-9210
The Trainer's Warehouse
  89 Washington Ave., Natick, MA 01760, 1-800-299-3770
U.S. Toy Company
  1227 E. 119th Street, Grandview, MO 64030,
  1-800-255-6124
Oriental Trading Company, Inc.
  P.O. Box 3407, Omaha, NE 68103, 1-800-228-2269

**R**eferences

Covey, Stephen. *Seven Habits of Highly Effective People*. New York: Simon & Shuster, 1989.

Holtzman, Gary. "Good Job—M&M® Game" in *Session Builders*. Harrisburg, PA: Training Resource Corporation, 1986.

James, W.B., & M.W. Galbraith. "Perceptual Learning Styles: Implications and Techniques for the Practitioner" in *Lifelong Learning* (January, 1985): 20–23.

Nelson, Bob. "I Am the Flag." Philadelphia, PA: KYW Newsradio.

Newstrom, John W., & Edward E. Scannell. *Games Trainers Play*. New York: McGraw-Hill, 1980.

Oppenheim, Lynn. *Studies of the Effects of the Use of Overhead Transparencies on Business Meetings*. Philadelphia, PA: Wharton Applied Research Center, Wharton School, University of Pennsylvania, 1981.

Pachter, Barbara, & Marjorie Brody. *Prentice-Hall Complete Business Etiquette Handbook*. Englewood Cliffs, NJ: Prentice-Hall, 1995.

Silberman, Mel, & Karen Lawson. *101 Ways to Make Training Active*. San Francisco: Pfeiffer & Company, 1995.

Slan, Joanna. *Using Stories and Humor: Grab Your Audience*. Needham Heights, MA: Allyn & Bacon, 1997.

Vogel, Douglas R., Gary W. Dickson, John Lehman, & Kent Shuart. *Persuasion and the Role of Visual Presentation Support: The UM/3M Study*. Minneapolis, MN: Management Information Systems Research Center, School of Management, University of Minnesota, 1986.

Wagner, Jane. *The Search for Signs of Intelligent Life in the Universe*. New York: HarperCollins, 1986.

Walters, Lilly. *Secrets of Successful Speakers*. New York: McGraw-Hill, 1993.

About Toastmasters International

If the thought of public speaking is enough to stop you dead in your tracks, it may have the same effect on your career.

While surveys report that public speaking is one of people's most dreaded fears, the fact remains that the inability to effectively deliver a clear thought in front of others can spell doom for professional progress. The person with strong communication skills has a clear advantage over tongue-tied colleagues—especially in a competitive job market.

Toastmasters International, a nonprofit educational organization, helps people conquer their pre-speech jitters. From one club started in Santa Ana, California, in 1924, the organization now has more than 170,000 members in 8,300 clubs in 62 countries.

How Does It Work?

A Toastmasters club is a "learn by doing" workshop in which men and women hone their communication and leadership skills in a friendly, supportive atmosphere. A typical club has 20 members who meet weekly or biweekly to practice public speaking techniques. Members, who pay approximately $35 in dues twice a year, learn by progressing through a series of 10 speaking assignments and being evaluated on their performance by their fellow club members. When finished with the basic speech manual, members can select from among 14 advanced programs that are geared toward specific career needs. Members also have the opportunity to develop and practice leadership skills by working in the High Performance Leadership Program.

Besides taking turns to deliver prepared speeches and evaluate those of other members, Toastmasters give impromptu talks on assigned topics, usually related to current events. They also develop listening skills, conduct meetings, learn parliamentary procedure and gain leadership experience by serving as club officers. But most importantly, they develop self-confidence from accomplishing what many once thought impossible.

The benefits of Toastmasters' proven and simple learning formula has not been lost on the thousands of corporations that sponsor in-house Toastmasters clubs as cost-efficient means of satisfying their employees' needs for communication training. Toastmasters clubs can be found in the U.S. Senate and the House of Representatives, as well as in a variety of community organizations, prisons, universities, hospitals, military bases, and churches.

How to Get Started

Most cities in North America have several Toastmasters clubs that meet at different times and locations during the week. If you are interested in forming or joining a club, call (714) 858-8255. For a listing of local clubs, call (800) WE-SPEAK, or write Toastmasters International, PO Box 9052, Mission Viejo, California 92690, USA. You can also visit our website at http://www.toastmasters.org.

As the leading organization devoted to teaching public speaking skills, we are devoted to helping you become more effective in your career and daily life.

Terrence J. McCann
Executive Director, Toastmasters International

Allyn & Bacon presents...
The Essence of Public Speaking Series

Endorsed by Toastmasters International

"These excellent books are ideal for [those] who want to offer practical ideas about the wonderful world of paid speaking... and are also ideal for those who want to speak to promote their professions, careers, or causes. The *Essence of Public Speaking* books are easy to understand, and simple to activate."

— Dottie Walters, President, Walters International Speakers Bureau, Publisher, Sharing Ideas Magazine for Speakers, and Author of Speak & Grow Rich

Choosing Powerful Words: Eloquence That Works, by Ronald Carpenter

"If you are serious about speaking, this book will be an invaluable aid."

Dilp R. Abayasekara, Ph.D., DTM, CEO Speakers Services Unlimited, Toastmasters International Accredited Speaker

Delivering Dynamic Presentations: Using Your Voice and Body for Impact, by Ralph Hillman

"This is not only a MUST READ, it is a MUST LIVE book."

Jan M. Roelofs, Communications Consultant

Involving Your Audience: Making It Active, by Karen Lawson

"This book is chock full of tips and techniques that can help turn any presentation into an interactive gold mine."

George Morrisey, CSP, CPAE, author of *Morrisey on Planning*

Speaking for Impact: Connecting with Every Audience, by Shirley Nice

" This is a MUST READ for any speaker that wants to speak from the inside out."

Terry Paulson, Ph.D., professional speaker on *Making Change Work* and 1998-1999 President, National Speakers Association

Motivating Your Audience: Speaking from the Heart, by Hanoch McCarty

"This book reflects Hanoch McCarty's many years of experience and his incredibly inventive mind."

Jack Canfield, co-author of *Chicken Soup for the Soul*

**See Inside Front Cover for a Complete Listing
of the Essence of Public Speaking Books**

Allyn & Bacon Order Form
The Essence of Public Speaking Series

NOW YOU CAN ORDER THE REST OF THE BOOKS IN THE SERIES!

New Books in the Series!

❑ *Speaking for Impact,* by Shirley E. Nice,
   Order # T7025-4, $14.95
❑ *Choosing Powerful Words,* by Ronald H. Carpenter,
   Order # T7124-5, $14.95
❑ *Delivering Dynamic Presentations,* by Ralph Hillman,
   Order # T6810-0, $14.95
❑ *Involving Your Audience,* by Karen Lawson,
   Order # T6811-8, $14.95
❑ *Motivating Your Audience,* by Hanoch McCarty,
   Order # T6894-4, $14.95

Previously Published Titles in the Series

❑ *Speaking for Profit and Pleasure,* by William D. Thompson,
   Order # T7026-2, $12.00
❑ *Speaking Your Way to the Top,* by Marjorie Brody,
   Order # T6814-2, $12.00
❑ *TechEdge,* by William J. Ringle,
   Order # T7305-0, $12.00
❑ *Using Stories and Humor,* by Joanna Slan,
   Order # T6893-6, $12.00
❑ *Writing Great Speeches,* by Alan Perlman,
   Order # T7300-1, $12.00

Name: _____

Address: _____

City: _____ State: _____ Zip: _____

Phone: _____ E-mail: _____

__Charge my   ___AMEX   ___VISA   ___Mastercard   ___Discover

Credit Card # _____ Exp. Date _____

MPG002   B1270A2-9

To place an order:

MAIL:
Allyn & Bacon Publishers
111 10th Street
Des Moines, IA 50309

CALL toll-free: 1-800-278-3525
FAX: 1-515-284-2607
WEBSITE: www.abacon.com